EUROPEAN COUNTRIES TODAY

UNITED KINGDOM

EUROPEAN COUNTRIES TODAY
TITLES IN THE SERIES

Austria	Italy
Belgium	Netherlands
Czech Republic	Poland
Denmark	Portugal
France	Spain
Germany	Sweden
Greece	United Kingdom
Ireland	European Union Facts & Figures

EUROPEAN COUNTRIES TODAY
UNITED KINGDOM

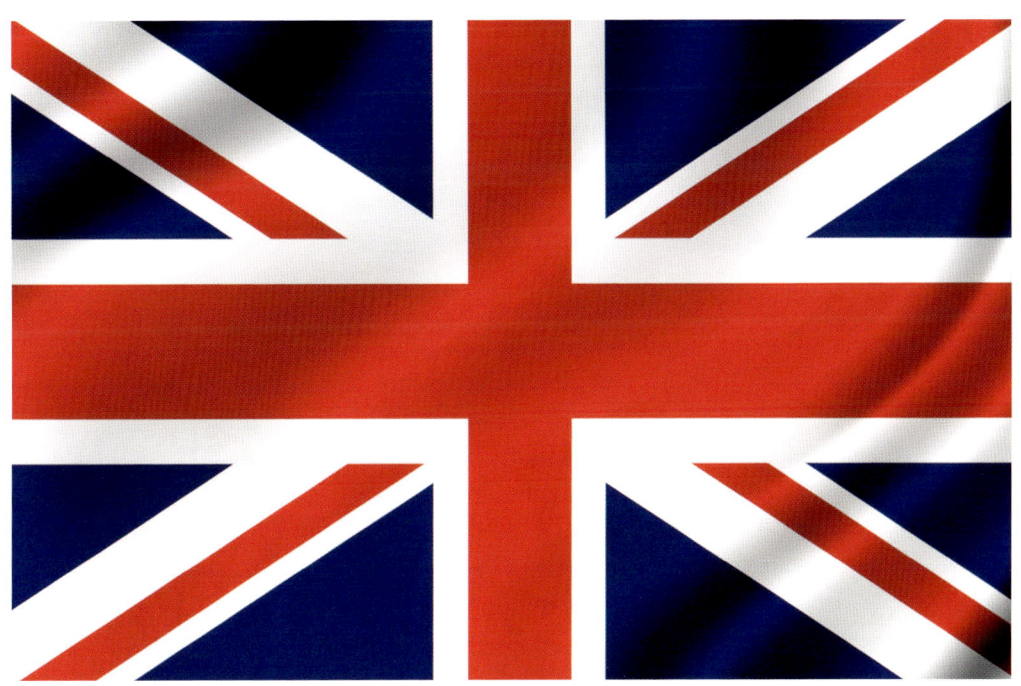

Dominic J. Ainsley

MASON CREST

Mason Crest
450 Parkway Drive, Suite D
Broomall, Pennsylvania PA 19008
(866) MCP-BOOK (toll free)

Copyright © 2019 by Mason Crest, an imprint of National Highlights, Inc. All rights reserved. No part of this publication may be reproduced or transmitted in any form or by any means, electronic or mechanical, including photocopying, recording, taping, or any information storage and retrieval system, without permission in writing from the publisher.

First printing
9 8 7 6 5 4 3 2 1

ISBN: 978-1-4222-3993-3
Series ISBN: 978-1-4222-3977-3
ebook ISBN: 978-1-4222-7808-6

Cataloging-in-Publication Data on file with the Library of Congress.

Printed in the United States of America

Cover images
Main: *Tenby, Wales.*
Left: *The Giant's Causeway, Northern Ireland.*
Center: *The Houses of Parliament, England.*
Right: *The Changing of the Guard, Buckingham Palace, England.*

QR CODES AND LINKS TO THIRD-PARTY CONTENT

You may gain access to certain third-party content ("Third- Party Sites") by scanning and using the QR Codes that appear in this publication (the "QR Codes"). We do not operate or control in any respect any information, products, or services on such Third-Party Sites linked to by us via the QR Codes included in this publication, and we assume no responsibility for any materials you may access using the QR Codes. Your use of the QR Codes may be subject to terms, limitations, or restrictions set forth in the applicable terms of use or otherwise established by the owners of the Third-Party Sites. Our linking to such Third-Party Sites via the QR Codes does not imply an endorsement or sponsorship of such Third-Party Sites or the information, products, or services offered on or through the Third-Party Sites, nor does it imply an endorsement or sponsorship of this publication by the owners of such Third-Party Sites.

CONTENTS

The United Kingdom at a Glance	6
Chapter 1: The United Kingdom's Geography & Landscape	11
Chapter 2: The Government & History of the United Kingdom	27
Chapter 3: The United Kingdom's Economy	49
Chapter 4: Citizens of the United Kingdom: People, Customs & Culture	59
Chapter 5: The Famous Cities of the United Kingdom	73
Chapter 6: A Bright Future for the United Kingdom	87
Chronology	90
Further Reading & Internet Resources	91
Index	92
Picture Credits & Author	96

KEY ICONS TO LOOK FOR:

Words to Understand: These words with their easy-to-understand definitions will increase the reader's understanding of the text while building vocabulary skills.

Sidebars: This boxed material within the main text allows readers to build knowledge, gain insights, explore possibilities, and broaden their perspectives by weaving together additional information to provide realistic and holistic perspectives.

Educational Videos: Readers can view videos by scanning our QR codes, providing them with additional content to supplement the text. Examples include news coverage, moments in history, speeches, iconic sports moments, and much more!

Text-Dependent Questions: These questions send the reader back to the text for more careful attention to the evidence presented there.

Research Projects: Readers are pointed toward areas of further inquiry connected to each chapter. Suggestions are provided for projects that encourage deeper research and analysis.

The Geography of the United Kingdom

Location: western Europe, islands including the northern one-sixth of the island of Ireland, between the North Atlantic Ocean and the North Sea, northwest of France

Area: (twice the size of Pennsylvania)
  total: 94,057 square miles (243,610 sq. km)
  land: 93,409 square miles (241,930 sq. km)
  water: 648 square miles (1,680 sq. km)

Borders: Republic of Ireland 275 miles (443 km)

Climate: temperate; moderated by prevailing southwest winds over the North Atlantic Current; more than half of the days are overcast

Terrain: mostly rugged hills and low mountains; level to rolling plains in east and southeast

Elevation extremes:
  lowest point: the Fens 13 feet (4 meters)
  highest point: Ben Nevis 4,406 feet (1,343 meters)

Natural hazards: winter windstorms; floods

Source: www.cia.gov 2017

THE UNITED KINGDOM AT A GLANCE

Flag of the United Kingdom

The United Kingdom of Great Britain and Northern Ireland is made up of England, Scotland, Wales, Northern Ireland, and many offshore islands. The country is situated on the westernmost edge of Europe and, despite being situated in a northerly position, has a temperate climate due to the North Atlantic Drift. The flag dates from 1603 and combines the crosses of St. George of England and St. Andrew of Scotland. The cross of St. Patrick of Ireland was added in 1801 to the make the flag as we know it today.

ABOVE: *Covent Garden, in central London, used to be a fruit and vegetable market. In the 1980s, it was redeveloped into an area of shops, restaurants, and bars.*

EUROPEAN COUNTRIES TODAY: UNITED KINGDOM

The People of the United Kingdom

Population: 64,769,452 (July 2017 est.)

Ethnic Groups: white 87.2%; black/African/Caribbean/black British 3%; Asian/Asian British: Indian 2.3%; Pakistani 1.9%; mixed 2%; other 3.7% (last census)

Age Structure:
- 0–14 years: 17.53%
- 15–24 years: 11.9%
- 25–54 years: 40.55%
- 55–64 years: 11.98%
- 65 years and above: 18.04% (2017 est.)

Population Growth Rate: 0.5% (2017 est.)

Birth Rate: 12.1 births/1,000 population (2017 est.)

Death Rate: 9.4 deaths/1,000 population (2017 est.)

Migration Rate: 2.5 migrant(s)/1,000 population (2017 est.)

Infant Mortality Rate: 4.3 deaths/1,000 live births

Life Expectancy at Birth:
- Total Population: 80.7 years
- Male: 78.5 years
- Female: 83 years (2016 est.)

Total Fertility Rate: 1.88 children born/woman (2017 est.)

Religions: Christian (includes Anglican, Roman Catholic, Presbyterian, Methodist) 59.5%, Muslim 4.4%, Hindu 1.3%, other 2%, unspecified 7.2%, none 25.7% (2011 est.)

Languages: the following are recognized regional languages: Scots (about 30% of the population of Scotland), Scottish Gaelic (about 60,000 in Scotland), Welsh (about 20% of the population of Wales), Irish (about 10% of the population of Northern Ireland), Cornish (some 2,000 to 3,000 in Cornwall)

Source: www.cia.gov 2017

Words to Understand

folklore: Traditional customs, beliefs, stories, and sayings.

moorland: An expanse of open, rolling, and infertile land.

mythology: The myths dealing with the gods, demigods, and legendary heroes of a particular people.

BELOW: Wastwater is one of many lakes in the Lake District National Park. The Lake District is in the county of Cumbria, in the northwest of England. The region also features England's highest mountain, Scafell Pike, at 3,209 feet (978 meters) above sea level.

Chapter One
THE UNITED KINGDOM'S GEOGRAPHY & LANDSCAPE

Almost everyone in North America has heard of King Arthur and his knights, and of Robin Hood, the Loch Ness Monster, Shakespeare, Ebenezer Scrooge, and pixies and brownies. These characters from history, literature, and **mythology** have helped shape North American **folklore**—but the roots of their stories lie deep in Britain's soil.

In many ways, Britain was the "mother" of large parts of North America. British immigrants settled throughout North America and brought their stories,

ABOVE: According to legend, Tintagel Castle on Cornwall's north coast is said to be the birthplace of King Arthur. Cornwall is located in southwest England.

11

THE UNITED KINGDOM'S GEOGRAPHY & LANDSCAPE

Educational Video

The difference between the United Kingdom, Great Britain, and England explained. Scan the QR code with your phone to watch!

their language, and their culture with them. Neither Canada nor the United States can truly understand their own identity without understanding the ancient land of Britain.

Today, Great Britain consists of four nations: England to the south, Scotland to the north, Wales to the west, and Northern Ireland across the North Channel on the island it shares with the Republic of Ireland. Collectively, they are known as the United Kingdom.

Rocks and Rivers, Mountains and Plains

Britain's land is truly ancient; the oldest rocks that form this island nation date back 2.6 billion years. This is the rugged foundation for the wild, mountainous scenery of Wales, Scotland, and Northern England. Because the United Kingdom is an island nation with a heavily indented coastline, wherever you are in Britain, you are no more than seventy-eight miles (125 kilometers) from the sea.

England

England's land is mostly low hills and plains, with a long, jagged coastline that is cut by bays, coves, and estuaries. If you could stretch the coastline out straight, it would cover 1,988 miles (3,200 kilometers). Mountains called the Pennines, England's backbone, split northern England into its western and

EUROPEAN COUNTRIES TODAY: UNITED KINGDOM

ABOVE: *Part of the Pennine Way footpath in North Yorkshire, England. In the distance is St. Margaret's Church, Hawes.*

THE UNITED KINGDOM'S GEOGRAPHY & LANDSCAPE

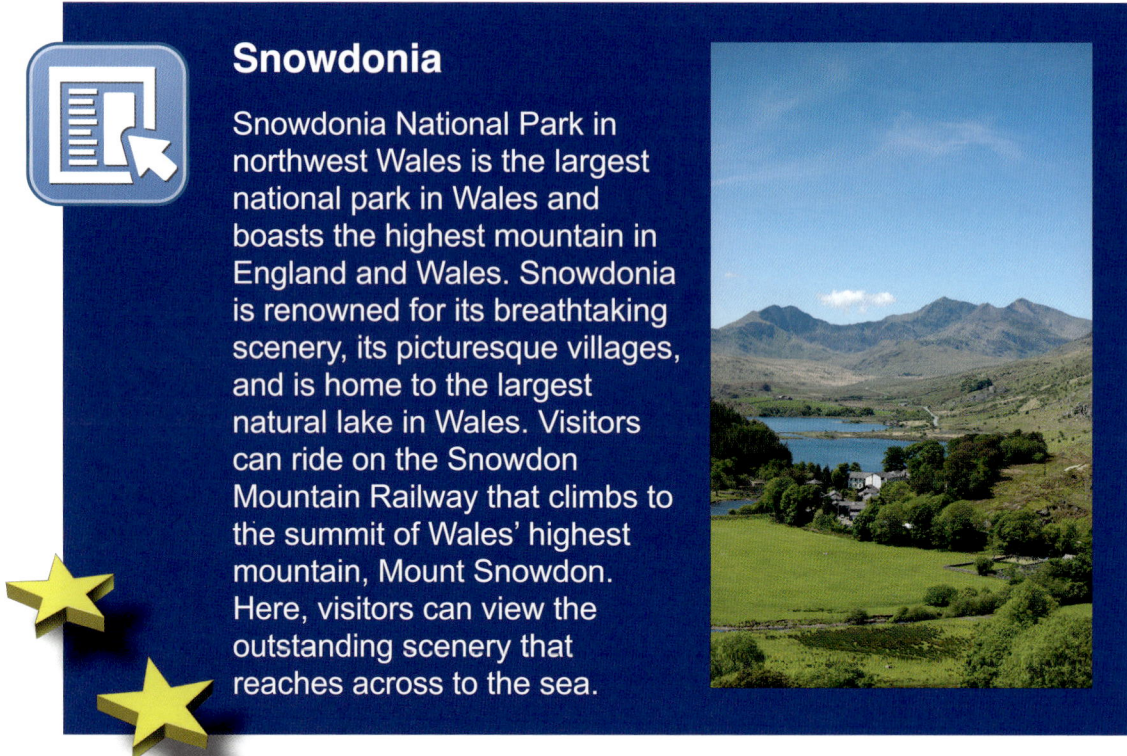

Snowdonia

Snowdonia National Park in northwest Wales is the largest national park in Wales and boasts the highest mountain in England and Wales. Snowdonia is renowned for its breathtaking scenery, its picturesque villages, and is home to the largest natural lake in Wales. Visitors can ride on the Snowdon Mountain Railway that climbs to the summit of Wales' highest mountain, Mount Snowdon. Here, visitors can view the outstanding scenery that reaches across to the sea.

eastern regions. England's highest peak is Scafell Pike (3,209 feet, or 978 meters) in the northwestern Lake District. The northeastern region includes the bleak but beautiful Yorkshire moors.

Wales

About one-quarter of the land of Wales is higher than 1,001 feet (305 meters). In the north, its highest peak, Snowdon (called Yr Wyddfa in Welsh), rises to 3,560 feet (1,085 meters). Just as in England, the Welsh coasts are cut by bays and extended by peninsulas.

Scotland

Along the border between Scotland and England, the Lowlands and Borderlands feature gently wooded hills. If you were to travel north, however, you would see a dramatic change as you entered the Highlands' rugged

EUROPEAN COUNTRIES TODAY: UNITED KINGDOM

ABOVE: Edinburgh Castle dominates the skyline of Edinburgh, Scotland. The castle stands upon the plug of an extinct volcano. The volcano was formed 350 million years ago.

THE UNITED KINGDOM'S GEOGRAPHY & LANDSCAPE

ABOVE: *The Jacobite Steam Train, of the West Coast Railways, crosses the Glenfinnan Viaduct that was made famous by the* Harry Potter *movies. Glenfinnan is a hamlet in the Lochaber area in the Highlands of Scotland. Today, the railroad is an important tourist attraction. It passes through an area of outstanding natural beauty.*

EUROPEAN COUNTRIES TODAY: UNITED KINGDOM

The Giant's Causeway

For hundreds of years, visitors have been intrigued by the mystical Giant's Causeway. It comprises 40,000 interlocking basalt columns, which are the result of ancient volcanic activity. The Giant's Causeway is located in County Antrim on the north coast of Northern Ireland. The location was included on the World Heritage site list by UNESCO in 1986.

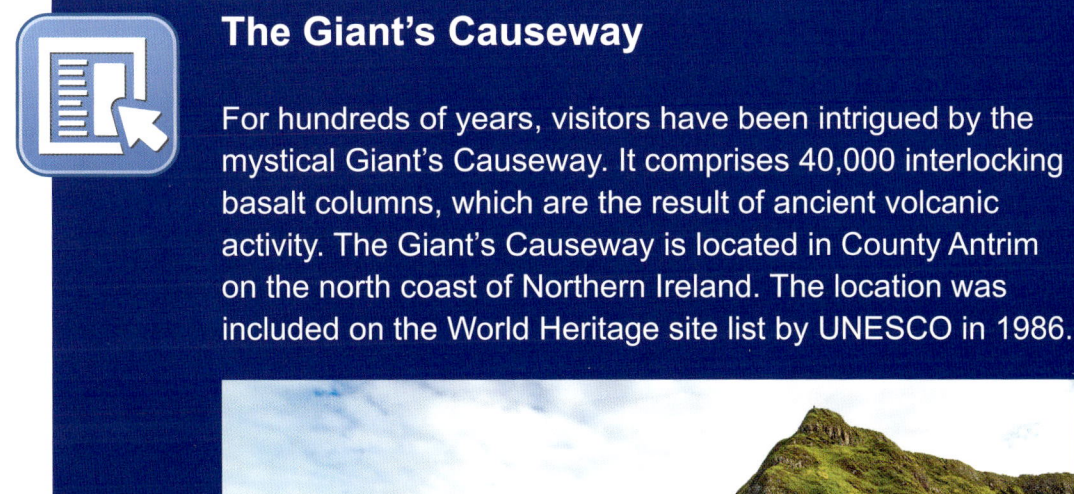

mountains. Glen More—the Great Glen—cuts across the central highlands, reaching from Fort William on the west coast all the way to Inverness on the east coast. Deep narrow lakes—called *lochs*—are strung between the steep mountains that rise above forested foothills to the high moors and rocky mountains. Scotland's Ben Nevis (4,403 feet, or 1,342 meters) is the highest point in the United Kingdom.

Northern Ireland

Northern Ireland and Scotland are separated from each other by the narrow North Channel, only thirteen miles (21 kilometers) wide at its narrowest point.

17

THE UNITED KINGDOM'S GEOGRAPHY & LANDSCAPE

ABOVE: *The mountains of Mourne are a granite mountain range in County Down, in the southeast of Northern Ireland. The highest mountains in the region can be found here. This beautiful area is popular with campers and walkers.*

To the south, Northern Ireland shares a 303-mile (488-kilometer) border with the Republic of Ireland, another member state of the European Union (EU). Northern Ireland's landscape is mostly made up of low green hills, but it also has two mountain ranges: the Mournes, which extend from South Down to Strangford Lough in the east, and the Sperrins in the northwest. Lough Neagh is the United Kingdom's largest body of fresh water, and is also one of the largest in all of Europe.

Britain's Climate

Although the United Kingdom lies further north than most of the United States, its climate is mild and temperate. At their extreme, temperatures rarely rise above 90 degrees Fahrenheit (32 degrees Celsius) in midsummer, and in the

EUROPEAN COUNTRIES TODAY: UNITED KINGDOM

winter they seldom drop below 14 degrees Fahrenheit (-10 degrees Celsius). Most of the time, however, temperatures range between 45 and 70 degrees Fahrenheit (7 and 21 degrees Celsius). The warm North Atlantic Current arcs around the United Kingdom, and prevailing southwest winds bring the current's warmth and moisture inland to the British Isles. The United Kingdom's four countries share four clearly marked seasons: spring (March through May), summer (June through August), fall (September through November), and winter (December through February). Rainfall is greatest in the mountains, where the yearly average is seventy-nine inches (2,000 millimeters); western and upland regions are also moist and rainy, with yearly average rainfalls of more than forty-three inches (1,100 millimeters). Meanwhile, across much of central England, the annual rainfall ranges from to twenty-eight to thirty-three inches (700 to 850 millimeters).

ABOVE: *Contrary to popular belief, it doesn't always rain in the United Kingdom. On sunny days it can get quite hot. During the summer, British people flood to many of the United Kingdom's beautiful beaches, such as this one in the town of Cromer, Norfolk, England.*

THE UNITED KINGDOM'S GEOGRAPHY & LANDSCAPE

ABOVE: *Bamford Edge, in the Peak District National Park, is a rugged area of outstanding scenery in northern England.*

Because the United Kingdom lies so far north, days are short during the winter months, but longer in the summer. During May, June, and July, when days are longest, the average hours of sunshine range from five hours in northern Scotland to eight hours further south on the Isle of Wight. During the winter months, when days are shortest, northern Scotland only gets an average of an hour a day of full sunlight, while the south coast of England has about two sunshine hours.

Over the centuries, Great Britain's islands have been nurtured and protected by the sea that surrounds them. The sea keeps winters mild, which in turn makes a longer growing season possible. This, plus the wet weather, make the country famously green.

EUROPEAN COUNTRIES TODAY: UNITED KINGDOM

Flora & Fauna

With its temperate climate and topography, the United Kingdom has a diverse pattern of natural vegetation. Originally, oak forests covered lowland areas, except for the fens and marshes. Pine forests and patches of **moorland** covered the higher or sandy ground. Over the centuries, however, much of the forested regions, especially on the lowlands, were cleared for farming. Today, only about 9 percent of the total surface is wooded. Fairly extensive forests remain in east and north Scotland, and in southeast England. Oak, ash, and

Eurasian Red Squirrel

This attractive squirrel mainly inhabits the woodland areas of northern England and Scotland. Red squirrels feed on shoots, pine cones, and other seeds, storing excess items in hollow trees or in holes in the ground. Stripped pine cones, scattered about the woodland floor, can point to the fact that the species has been active. The red squirrel's nest is known as a dray, which is a relatively small, compact structure. Red squirrels produce one or two litters of about three young each year. The red squirrel has sharp claws, and consequently, is very good at climbing. Its curved claws enable it to climb and descend both large and small trees. With strong hind legs, it excels at leaping between gaps in the trees. The red squirrel also has the ability to swim. Red squirrels that survive their first winter have a life expectancy of three years.

21

THE UNITED KINGDOM'S GEOGRAPHY & LANDSCAPE

ABOVE: *The New Forest National Park is in Hampshire, England. It is an area of ancient forest and heathland, where horses and cattle roam freely, along with deer and pigs.*

EUROPEAN COUNTRIES TODAY: UNITED KINGDOM

beech are the most common trees in England. Pine and birch are most common in Scotland. Nowadays, virtually all the lowland areas outside the towns and cities are farmland. These areas support varied seminatural vegetation, including grasses and flowering plants. Wild vegetation consists of the natural flora of woods, fens and marshes, cliffs, chalk downs, and mountain slopes, the most widespread being the heather, grasses, gorse, and bracken of the moorlands.

ABOVE: *The Fens are an area of reclaimed land in the east of England that, in most cases, are barely above sea level. This fertile land is interlaced with rivers and drainage ditches, some dating back to Roman times. The Fens are home to a good deal of wildlife, such as otters, water voles, herons, bitterns, and hen harriers.*

THE UNITED KINGDOM'S GEOGRAPHY & LANDSCAPE

ABOVE: *The Farne Islands are situated off the coast of Northumberland, in the northeast of England. Many are uninhabited. The islands are important breeding grounds for many seabirds, including puffins (shown above), guillemots, and arctic terns.*

Britain is home to a variety of mammals, reptiles, and amphibians. However, compared with reptiles and amphibians, Britain is quite well endowed with mammals, and its seventy or more mammalian species make it a rich and varied group. They include the night-hunting bats and hedgehogs, the grazing land herbivores, such as the deer and rabbits, the carnivorous hunters, such as foxes and stoats, the aquatic water voles and otters, and the marine dwellers that include seals and whales. By comparison, Britain has only six native reptiles and the same number of native amphibians. There are several reasons for this: because of their fur-covered bodies, mammals are better suited to the cool climate and terrain (originally woodland, although much of it was eventually cleared by human beings for farming). By contrast, reptiles and amphibians are cold-blooded, meaning that their body temperature varies with that of their environment, leading them to prefer warmer climates further south.

EUROPEAN COUNTRIES TODAY: UNITED KINGDOM

ABOVE: *Hedgehogs are widespread throughout the United Kingdom. They are a much loved and appealing species. In the last decade, their numbers have declined rapidly. This is thought to be due to modern farming practices and the use of pesticides.*

Text-Dependent Questions

1. Which nations make up the United Kingdom?

2. Where is Snowdonia National Park?

3. How far is Northern Ireland from Scotland?

Research Project

Describe a temperate climate. Explain how the United Kingdom's location influences its climate.

Words to Understand

archaeologists: Scientists who deal with past human life and activities as shown by objects (as pottery, tools, and statues) left by ancient peoples.

glaciers: Large bodies of ice that move slowly down a slope or over a wide area of land.

Stone Age: The oldest period in which human beings are known to have existed. The age during which stone tools were used.

BELOW: Stonehenge is a prehistoric monument on Salisbury Plain in Wiltshire, England. It comprises a ring of standing stones. Each one is approximately 13 feet (4.1 meters) high and 6 feet 11 inches (2.1 meters) wide. The site dates from around 3100 BCE. The stones were sourced and then brought from Wales in an amazing feat of determination and engineering.

Chapter Two
THE GOVERNMENT & HISTORY OF THE UNITED KINGDOM

More than 800,000 years ago, the first **Stone Age** people settled the land that is now the United Kingdom. At that time, however, the land was not an island; in fact, the British Isles were not separated from the rest of Europe until 8,500 years ago, when melting **glaciers** formed the English Channel that today separates England from France.

About three thousand years after Britain became an island, new tribes came by boat from the mainland. They built forts and tombs made of earth; many of these ancient manmade hills and mounds can still be seen across the British Isles.

Centuries later, when Britain's climate abruptly became both colder and wetter, its inhabitants moved down from higher ground to the lowlands. About five hundred years later, a new wave of immigrants—the Celts—started to arrive from southern Europe. They may have brought with them a new technology: ironworking.

Historians don't know very much about these half-forgotten people. What they do know comes from information **archaeologists** have pieced together from the objects left behind by Britain's first people. Not until more than two thousand years after Stonehenge's first stones were erected did someone come to the British Isles who could read and write: Pytheas, a Greek who traveled there around 330 BCE. Most of Pytheas's writings have been lost, so the first written records we have of Britain are when the Romans arrived, almost three hundred years after Pytheas.

THE GOVERNMENT & HISTORY OF THE UNITED KINGDOM

The Roman Invasion

In 55 BCE, Julius Caesar's troops invaded the British Isles. Caesar was hoping to gain gold, silver, and tin from Britain, but victory did not come easily. Although his well-trained armies did win some battles, the wild seas around the islands proved to be formidable, and, again and again, Caesar's ships were wrecked by storms.

Not until a century later, in 43 CE, did the Romans manage to bring the British Isles into their empire. This time the Roman emperor sent 40,000 soldiers, some of them mounted on elephants. The British had never seen such animals, and they were terrified!

For almost four hundred years—nearly twice as long as the United States has been a nation—the Roman Empire ruled Britain. During that time, Britain

Dating Systems and Their Meaning

You might be accustomed to seeing dates expressed with the abbreviations BC or AD, as in the year 1000 BC or the year AD 1900. For centuries, this dating system has been the most common in the Western world. However, since BC and AD are based on Christianity (BC stands for Before Christ and AD stands for anno Domini, Latin for "in the year of our Lord"), many people now prefer to use abbreviations that people from all religions can be comfortable using. The abbreviations BCE (meaning Before Common Era) and CE (meaning Common Era), mark time in the same way (for example, 1000 BC is the same year as 1000 BCE, and AD 1900 is the same year as 1900 CE), but BCE and CE do not have the same religious overtones as BC and AD.

EUROPEAN COUNTRIES TODAY: UNITED KINGDOM

ABOVE: *Hadrian's Wall, built in the reign of the emperor Hadrian, was a defensive fortification started in 122 CE and finished six years later. It was constructed by 15,000 workers. It stretched from the banks of the river Tyne near the North Sea to the Solway Firth on the Irish Sea. The wall marked the northern limit of the Roman Empire, with its purpose to protect Roman Britain from the Picts in the north.*

THE GOVERNMENT & HISTORY OF THE UNITED KINGDOM

had more contact with the rest of Europe than it had ever had before. The Romans' stable government brought peace and culture. They also built a system of roads, many of which are still in use. The remains of their buildings and baths can be seen across the United Kingdom.

But no empire lasts forever, and in 410, the weakened Roman Empire withdrew from Britain. The peaceful inhabitants who remained behind were left with no strong army to protect them.

ABOVE: *Alfred the Great died in Winchester, England, which is where this statue is located.*

The Invasion of the Anglo-Saxons

The tribes of Denmark, northern Germany, and Holland (called the Angles, the Jutes, and the Saxons) realized that the islands were vulnerable. Their own land was poor and often flooded, and they were looking for new places to live and farm. Anglo-Saxon families rowed across the North Sea in wooden boats and formed small settlements in Britain. Eventually, they ruled over most of it, although they never conquered Wales and Cornwall in the west or Scotland in the north. The Anglo-Saxon king, Alfred the Great, was the first ruler to control most of England. In 597 CE, St. Augustine came to Britain as a missionary from Rome, and the Anglo-Saxons gradually converted to Christianity.

The Normans

For centuries, Vikings had been sweeping down from the north to raid the European lands to the south. Britain bore its share of these raids, as did France across the English Channel. Around the year 1000, a

EUROPEAN COUNTRIES TODAY: UNITED KINGDOM

group of Vikings—called "North Men" or "Normans"—settled in France in the area that is now known as Normandy. The Normans became Christians, but as the generations passed, some of them grew tired of farming and wanted the adventures and riches of their grandfathers.

In 1066, William, Duke of Normandy, sailed across the English Channel and conquered the Anglo-Saxons. William became the new king of England. He built many castles, where his nobles lived, and he made French the official language. For many years, both French and Anglo-Saxon were spoken across Britain. (The English that is spoken today, however, has more roots in Anglo-Saxon than it does in French.) William the Conqueror, like his son and grandson, was a strong king who brought stable rule once again to Britain.

William the Conqueror's great-grandson, King John, however, did not get along well with the nobles. In 1215, they rebelled and forced him to sign the Magna Carta—Latin for "Great Charter"—a document that would form the foundation for Britain's (and later, Canada's and America's) government.

The Middle Ages

The years that followed were unsettled for the English royals, with many contending for the throne. William's son, William II,

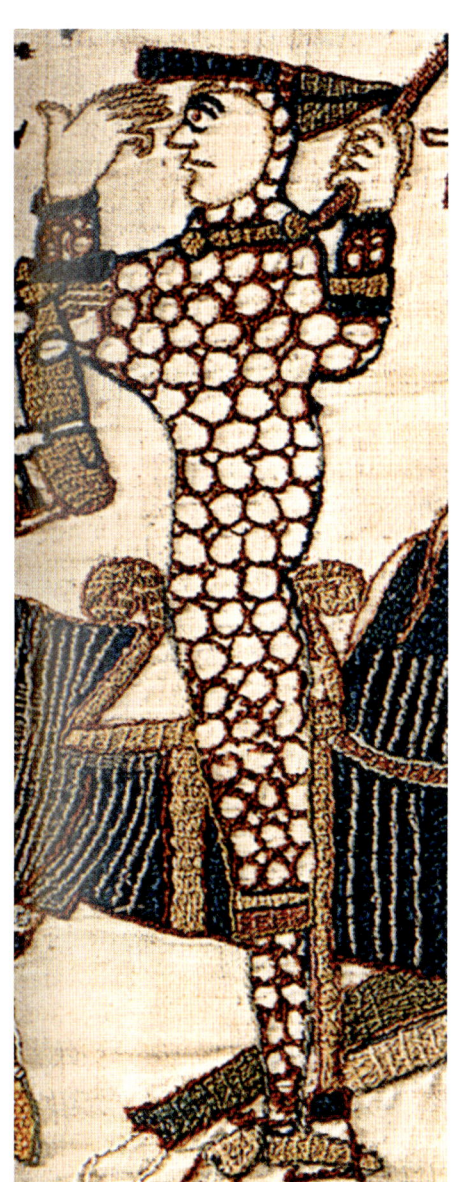

ABOVE: William the Conqueror during the Battle of Hastings, as depicted in a segment of the Bayeux Tapestry. He lifts his helmet to show others that he is still alive.

was killed in an accident in the hunting field, although it is now believed that he was murdered so that William's second son, Henry, could become king. Henry I's succession was also marked by turbulent times, with his daughter Matilda and her cousin Stephen (grandson of William I) instigating a civil war to gain the throne. Eventually Stephen won, however, it was Matilda's son who ultimately became king, becoming Henry II (1133–89). Henry II had two children, Richard "Lionheart" and John Lackland, who also battled for the throne. It was Richard, the eldest son who eventually succeeded his father. Richard was rarely in England for he was fighting wars in foreign lands, either defending his French possessions or fighting in the Holy Land. His brother John Lackland muscled in, took the throne and started another civil war. John's grandson Edward I, also known as Edward Longshanks (1239–1307) spent most of his reign fighting wars, including one against the Scots, who were led by William Wallace and Robert the Bruce. With these two strong leaders, the Scots were able to resist the English. However, William Wallace was captured by the English and executed in 1305.

ABOVE: *A statue of Robert the Bruce, king of Scotland, at Stirling Castle, Scotland.*

The Rise of the Tudors

In the fifteenth century, civil wars called the Wars of the Roses threatened to tear apart Britain's peaceful countryside. A white rose was the badge of the Yorkists, while their opponents, the Lancastrians, wore a red rose as their symbol. Both sides' leaders had royal blood, and both claimed the throne. Across Britain, the nobles took one side or another, and battles raged for thirty years. The fighting finally ended in 1485

EUROPEAN COUNTRIES TODAY: UNITED KINGDOM

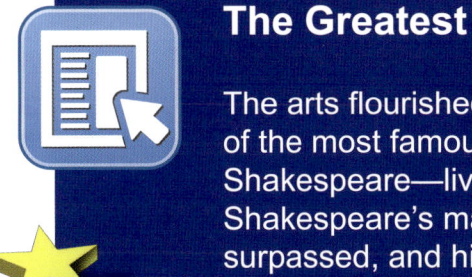

The Greatest Author in the World

The arts flourished during Elizabeth I's peaceful reign. One of the most famous writers of all time—William Shakespeare—lived during the time Elizabeth was queen. Shakespeare's mastery of English has never been surpassed, and his plays and poetry continue to be enjoyed by people around the world.

when the York king was defeated. A Welshman, Henry VII, the first of the line of kings called the Tudors, took the throne and brought peace back to Britain.

Henry's son was Henry VIII, famous both for his many wives and for starting the Anglican Church, which still exists. After his death, his daughter Elizabeth eventually took the throne, becoming one of England's greatest monarchs. During her reign, Britain's power grew, and its influence extended across the seas, all the way to North America, where her adventurers sailed. Because Elizabeth I never married, she was known as the Virgin Queen; the American state of Virginia was named after her.

These were eventful years in Britain's history. During the reign of Elizabeth's cousin James, in 1620, the Pilgrims set

ABOVE: *King Henry VIII is England's most famous and infamous king.*

33

THE GOVERNMENT & HISTORY OF THE UNITED KINGDOM

ABOVE: *Charles II was king of Great Britain and Ireland (1660–85). He reigned during a difficult period of struggles between Anglicans, Catholics, and dissenters. His wisdom and knowledge enabled him to steer his country through those challenging times.*

EUROPEAN COUNTRIES TODAY: UNITED KINGDOM

sail for New England aboard the Mayflower. As Britain's power at home grew, its people also traveled far across the ocean and began settling the "New World." Kings came and went, while the British people prospered, both on their island home and across the oceans in their many colonies around the world.

The House of Stuart

The Stuarts can be traced back to eleventh-century Brittany, France. By the early twelfth century, they appeared in England. From 1371–1603 there were nine Stuart monarchs who ruled Scotland. During this time, Scotland developed from a relatively poor and feudal country into a prosperous, modern and centralized state. When the childless Tudor Queen Elizabeth I died in 1603, James I and VI (1603–25), son of Mary, Queen of Scots and Henry Stuart, became the first joint ruler of the kingdoms of England and Scotland. During her residence in France, Mary, Queen of Scots, changed the spelling of the ancient Scottish dynasty from Stewart to Stuart.

From the Stuart Reign until Today

While maintaining separate parliaments, England and Scotland were ruled under one crown beginning in 1603, when James IV of Scotland succeeded his cousin Elizabeth I as James I of England. In the century that followed, strong religious and political differences divided the kingdoms. Finally, in 1707, England and Scotland were unified as Great Britain, sharing a single parliament at Westminster. Nearly three hundred years later, in July 1999, power to administer Scottish affairs was given to a new Scottish parliament.

35

🇬🇧 **THE GOVERNMENT & HISTORY OF THE UNITED KINGDOM**

The House of Hanover
In 1714, Queen Anne, Britain's last Stuart monarch, died. The crown of England was then passed by the 1701 Act of Settlement to the Stuart dynasty's German Protestant cousins, the House of Hanover. This act only allowed succession to English and Irish crowns by Protestants only. The House of Hanover provided monarchs to Great Britain and Ireland from 1714 until 1901, when Queen Victoria died. Upon her death the throne was passed to her eldest son, Edward VII.

The Victorian Age
By the nineteenth century, Britain had formed an empire. So many British colonies were spread around the globe that people said: "The sun never sets on the British Empire." In other words, somewhere on the globe, the sun was shining on one British colony or another. Although the American colonies were now their own nation, Canada, Australia, New Zealand, India, and much of Africa and the Middle and Far East were all part of this far-spread empire.

Queen Victoria ruled during these years of British power and influence. She took the throne in 1837, when she was only eighteen, and she reigned for more than sixty-three years—longer than any other British king or queen. Her personality shaped not only Britain but the entire world.

A quarter of the entire world's population lived under Victoria's rule, and she built Britain into the greatest trading empire the world had ever known. The empire's administrators genuinely believed that they were helping the people they ruled; for instance, they abolished slavery throughout their colonies and brought education, law, democracy, and sports to the countries they governed. The native people of the colonies, however, were not always compliant, and historians still debate whether the British Empire was good for its colonies.

During Victoria's years on the throne, Britain was a leader in the industrial revolution. Goods that were once made by hand were now made in factories by machines. More and more people moved away from their farms and turned to the cities for jobs. London became the largest city in the world. Britain was the manufacturing leader of the world—but its workers paid the price with terrible living and working conditions.

EUROPEAN COUNTRIES TODAY: UNITED KINGDOM

ABOVE: Queen Victoria on her horse Fyvie, with John Brown, her personal attendant, at Balmoral Castle in Scotland.

🇬🇧 THE GOVERNMENT & HISTORY OF THE UNITED KINGDOM

Although Queen Victoria had tremendous influence, Parliament was actually in charge of the country during her reign, and British citizens gained most of the rights common in a democracy. Working people began fighting for better conditions and fairer pay.

ABOVE: *Balmoral Castle in Aberdeenshire, Scotland, was commissioned by Queen Victoria and was her favorite residence. Today, it is also a favorite of Queen Elizabeth II. Unlike Buckingham Palace or Windsor Castle, Balmoral is a private family estate, where the royals can enjoy privacy.*

EUROPEAN COUNTRIES TODAY: UNITED KINGDOM

ABOVE: British soliders marching in Mesopotamia during World War I in 1917. It was a war that took 18 million lives.

The Modern Age

By the time of Queen Victoria's death in 1901, other nations, including the United States, had developed their own manufacturing factories. Although Britain was a world leader during the battles of World War I, the war's losses and destruction, combined with the Depression of the 1930s, eroded the United Kingdom's international leadership.

At the same time, Britain's control over its empire loosened during the years between the world wars. Ireland, with the exception of six northern counties, gained independence from the United Kingdom in 1921. Nationalism became stronger in other parts of the empire, especially in India and Egypt.

THE GOVERNMENT & HISTORY OF THE UNITED KINGDOM

ABOVE: *The Yalta Conference was held in February 1945. Attending the conference were Winston Churchill, Franklin D. Roosevelt, and Joseph Stalin (seated above).*

In 1926, the United Kingdom granted Australia, Canada, and New Zealand complete autonomy within the empire. These nations became charter members of the British Commonwealth of Nations (now known as the Commonwealth). Beginning with the independence of India and Pakistan in 1947, the remainder of the British Empire was almost completely dismantled. Today, most of Britain's former colonies belong to the Commonwealth, almost all of them as independent members. However, thirteen former British colonies—including Bermuda, Gibraltar, and the Falkland Islands, and others—have

EUROPEAN COUNTRIES TODAY: UNITED KINGDOM

chosen to continue their links with the United Kingdom; they are known as United Kingdom Overseas Territories.

During World War II, Britain fought heroically against the Axis forces, but the war took a heavy toll on British cities, resources, and human life. Great Britain's culture was forever changed. When the war was finally over, the British people voted for a Labour government, and the National Health Service was introduced. This gave free health care to everyone, paid for by people's taxes.

Today, the United Kingdom's major political parties are Labour and Conservative. Margaret Thatcher, who led the Conservative Party, became Britain's first-ever woman prime minister in 1979. She was prime minister until 1990. John Major followed her, and then in 1997, Tony Blair took over, followed by Gordon Brown in 2009, and then David Cameron in 2010. The current prime minister is Theresa May, who succeeded David Cameron in 2016.

ABOVE: Aneurin Bevan was a Labour government minister. He was the chief architect of the National Health Service—the state-funded health service of the UK.

All throughout the twentieth century, Britain was America's closest ally, and that partnership continues into the twenty-first century. Troops from the two countries worked together to overthrow Saddam Hussein, and they continued to work to stabilize Iraq.

The United Kingdom's Government

The United Kingdom does not have a written constitution. Instead, its government is based on common law and traditional rights. Changes may come about formally through new acts of Parliament, informally through the acceptance of new practices and usage, or by judicial precedents. Although

THE GOVERNMENT & HISTORY OF THE UNITED KINGDOM

ABOVE: *The first woman prime minster, Margaret Thatcher.*

Parliament has the theoretical power to make or repeal any law, in actual practice the weight of seven hundred years of tradition acts as a restraint against any arbitrary actions.

Executive government rests in name only with the monarch; actually, it is controlled by a committee of ministers (a cabinet), traditionally selected from among the members of the House of Commons and, to a lesser extent, the House of Lords. The prime minister is normally the leader of the political party with the most members in the Commons, and the government is dependent on the leading party's support.

ABOVE: *The House of Commons is where the United Kingdom's government proposes and passes laws.*

EUROPEAN COUNTRIES TODAY: UNITED KINGDOM

ABOVE: *The iconic Houses of Parliament, seat of the United Kingdom's government, are located in London on the banks of the river Thames.*

Parliament represents the entire country and can legislate for the whole or for any part, or combination of parts. The maximum parliamentary term is five years, but the prime minister may ask the monarch to dissolve Parliament and call a general election at any time. The focus of legislative power is the 650-member House of Commons, which has sole jurisdiction over finance. The House of Lords, although shorn of most of its powers, can still review, amend, or delay temporarily any bills, except those relating to the budget. In 1999, the government removed the automatic right of hereditary peers to hold seats in the

THE GOVERNMENT & HISTORY OF THE UNITED KINGDOM

House of Lords. The Lords currently consists of appointed life peers, who hold their seats for life, and ninety-two hereditary peers, who will hold their seats only until final reforms have been agreed on and implemented.

The judiciary branch of the government is independent of the legislative and executive branches, but cannot review the legitimacy of legislation passed by the legislative branch.

This system of government was born out of Britain's long and ancient history. Today, it is the foundation for the United Kingdom's role in the modern world—and Britain's economy is built on it as well.

ABOVE: *Prime Minister Theresa May outside Downing Street, London.*

ABOVE: *10 Downing Street, London, is where the prime minister's residence and offices are located.*

EUROPEAN COUNTRIES TODAY: UNITED KINGDOM

ABOVE: Queen Elizabeth II and the royal family on the balcony at Buckingham Palace, celebrating the queen's birthday on June 13, 2015.

Text-Dependent Questions

1. When did the Romans invade the British Isles?

2. When did Queen Victoria die?

3. Who was the first king to rule over both England and Scotland?

Research Project

Write a short essay on the United Kingdom's parliamentary system.

THE GOVERNMENT & HISTORY OF THE UNITED KINGDOM

The Formation of the European Union (EU)

The EU is a confederation of European nations that continues to grow. As of 2017, there are twenty-eight official members. Several other candidates are also waiting for approval. All countries that enter the EU agree to follow common laws about foreign security policies. They also agree to cooperate on legal matters that go on within the EU. The European Council meets to discuss all international matters and make decisions about them. Each country's own concerns and interests are important, though. And apart from legal and financial issues, the EU tries to uphold values such as peace, human dignity, freedom, and equality.

All member countries remain autonomous. This means that they generally keep their own laws and regulations. The idea for a union among European nations was first mentioned after World War II. The war had devastated much of Europe, both physically and financially. In 1950, the French foreign minister suggested that France and West Germany combine their coal and steel industries under one authority. Both countries would have control over the

ABOVE: The entrance to the European Union Parliament Building in Brussels.

EUROPEAN COUNTRIES TODAY: UNITED KINGDOM

Member Countries

Austria	Greece	Romania
Belgium	Hungary	Slovakia
Bulgaria	Ireland	Slovenia
Croatia	Italy	Spain
Cyprus	Latvia	Sweden
Czech Republic	Lithuania	United Kingdom
Denmark	Luxembourg	*(Brexit: For the time*
Estonia	Malta	*being, the United*
Finland	Netherlands	*Kingdom remains a full*
France	Poland	*member of the EU.)*
Germany	Portugal	

industries. This would help them become more financially stable. It would also make war between the countries much more difficult. The idea was interesting to other European countries as well. In 1951, France, West Germany, Belgium, Luxembourg, the Netherlands, and Italy signed the Treaty of Paris, creating the European Coal and Steel Community. These six countries would become the core of the EU.

In 1957, these same countries signed the Treaties of Rome, creating the European Economic Community. In 1965, the Merger Treaty formed the European Community. Finally, in 1992, the Maastricht Treaty was signed. This treaty defined the European Union. It gave a framework for expanding the EU's political role, particularly in the area of foreign and security policy. It would also replace national currencies with the euro. The next year, the treaty went into effect. At that time, the member countries included the original six plus another six who had joined during the 1970s and '80s.

In the following years, the EU would take more steps to form a single market for its members. This would make joining the union even more advantageous. In addition to enlargement, the EU is steadily becoming more integrated through its own policies for closer cooperation between member states.

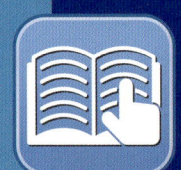

Words to Understand

labor unions: Organizations formed by workers to help them get better pay, protection, and working conditions.

legacy: Memories or knowledge that comes from the past or a person of the past.

recessions: Periods of reduced business activity or temporary economic depressions.

BELOW: The City of London is the United Kingdom's center for banking and finance. The Bank of England and the London Stock Exchange are situated there.

Chapter Three
THE UNITED KINGDOM'S ECONOMY

The United Kingdom is one Europe's great trading powers, and it is also an international finance center. Britain's long years as a world power have also left it with a **legacy** of influence in the business world. London, its capital, is an important trading center, used by other nations throughout the world.

Socialism has been a strong factor in the United Kingdom's economy; in other words, many businesses are public rather than private. The government uses heavy taxes to provide services to all segments of the society, no matter

ABOVE: *Grangemouth Refinery in Scotland, located on the Firth of Forth, is the only oil refinery in Scotland that refines North Sea oil.*

THE UNITED KINGDOM'S ECONOMY

how rich or poor. In the 1980s, however, the government reduced public ownership and put a limit on the growth of social welfare programs. Despite this trend, the Labour Party, which consists of **labor unions** and socialist societies, was able to put its leader, Tony Blair, into the prime minister's office in 1997 with a landslide victory. Yet with the recent **recessions**, the UK's government is once again swinging back to the policies of the 1980s, and placing greater limits on government spending. Austerity measures have been implemented in

ABOVE: London is the capital city of the United Kingdom and one of the world's leading business and financial centers. It contributes significantly to the economy of the country.

EUROPEAN COUNTRIES TODAY: UNITED KINGDOM

ABOVE: *The United Kingdom is rich in culture and steeped in history. This sixteenth-century house in Stratford-upon-Avon is believed to be the birthplace of William Shakespeare.*

order to rebalance the economy. However, despite the cuts in spending, the UK deficit still remains one of the highest in the G7. Britain's debt burden was 92.2 percent of the country's gross domestic product (GDP) at the end of 2016. Fortunately, recent reports show that the United Kingdom has one of the fastest growing economies in the G7, but there is concern about the potential impact of the country's vote to leave the EU. A breakdown of trading relationships with other EU members through its single market membership could affect the economy. There is also concern that London's status as a global financial center could also be jeopardized, and there is evidence that some of London's banks are considering relocating to Frankfurt in Germany, which is already home to the European Central Bank.

THE UNITED KINGDOM'S ECONOMY

ABOVE: Tata Steel Plant, Port Talbot, South Wales, is very important to the economy of Wales. In recent years, it has been under threat of closure, following cheap imports of steel from China.

The Foundation of Britain's Economy

The United Kingdom has large coal, natural gas, and oil reserves; these resources provide the economy with a strong foundation. Primary energy production accounts for a significant percentage of the GDP, and one of the highest percentages of any industrial nation.

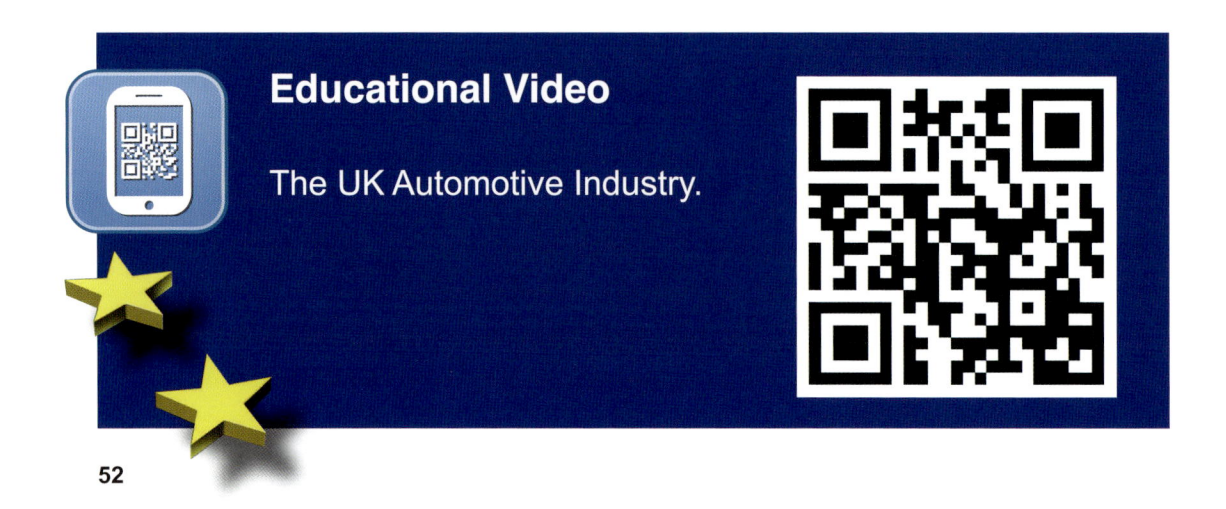

Educational Video

The UK Automotive Industry.

EUROPEAN COUNTRIES TODAY: UNITED KINGDOM

Service industries, particularly banking, insurance, and business services, account for the largest proportion of Britain's GDP, while industry has declined in importance.

Although the United Kingdom is a relatively small island with many urban centers, farming continues to be important to its economy. Its agriculture is highly mechanized and efficient, producing about half of its population's food

ABOVE: *The United Kingdom is renowned for its beautiful scenery. This is an arable farm in Shropshire, England, near the border with Wales.*

THE UNITED KINGDOM'S ECONOMY

needs with only 1 percent of the nation's labor force. However, the 1986 discovery of mad cow disease among its beef cattle, and a foot-and-mouth disease outbreak in 2001, shook the United Kingdom's farming industry. The nation, united with the rest of the EU, took courageous measures to control the crisis. Today, the UK's beef industry has recovered well, but still faces challenges.

An Island of Pounds in the Midst of Euros

Most of the EU now uses the euro as its currency—but not the United Kingdom. Some politicians have pushed for Britain's conversion, but the nation's good economic performance has complicated some of the arguments to make a case for Britain to join the European Economic and Monetary Union (EMU). Critics

ABOVE: About half of the United Kingdom's food is home-produced. Traditional British crops, such as brassicas, are produced locally, while other more exotic foods are imported.

EUROPEAN COUNTRIES TODAY: UNITED KINGDOM

The Economy of the United Kingdom

Gross Domestic Product (GDP): $2.785 trillion (2016 est.)
GDP Per Capita: $42,500 (2016 est.)
Industries: machine tools, electric power equipment, automation equipment, railroad equipment, shipbuilding, aircraft, motor vehicles and parts, electronics and communications equipment, metals, chemicals, coal, petroleum, paper and paper products, food processing, textiles, clothing, other consumer goods
Agriculture: cereals, oilseed, potatoes, vegetables, cattle, sheep, poultry, fish
Export Commodities: manufactured goods, fuels, chemicals, food, beverages, tobacco
Export Partners: US 14.8%, Germany 10.7%, France 6.4%, Netherlands 6.2%, Ireland 5.6%, Switzerland 4.6%, China 4.4% (2016)
Import Commodities: manufactured goods, machinery, fuels, foodstuffs
Import Partners: Germany 13.6%, US 9.3%, China 9.2%, Netherlands 7.4%, France 5.2%, Belgium 4.9%, Switzerland 4.5% (2016)
Currency: pound sterling

Source: www.cia.gov 2017

have pointed out that the British economy has done fine outside of the EMU, and public opinion polls have shown that a majority of Britons oppose the euro.

The momentum of Britain's thriving economy pushed it through more than ten years of steady growth into the twenty-first century. In the first decade of the new century, the nation also had lower unemployment rates than any other industrial nation. What's more, Britain invested more of its money in the United States than any other country during this period, so its healthy economy also gave jobs to more than a million Americans.

🇬🇧 THE UNITED KINGDOM'S ECONOMY

Brexit

The people of Britain voted for a prospective British withdrawal, or Brexit, from the EU in a historic referendum held on Thursday June 23, 2016.

The outcome prompted mass celebrations among Eurosceptics around the whole of Europe and sent shockwaves through the global economy. After the declaration of the referendum result, the pound fell to its lowest level since 1985 and David Cameron resigned as prime minister.

Eurosceptics believe that a successful Brexit will boost the UK's economy and increase trade with other countries outside the EU.

The 2008 Global Financial Crisis

In 2008, the entire world went into a recession—a period when businesses and finance stopped growing. Inflation rose, unemployment increased, and individuals and businesses alike struggled to keep their finances afloat. Because the economies of countries all around the world are so interlinked, especially within the EU, the world's money problems snowballed, becoming worse and worse over the next couple of years.

It works the other way around too, though: as the countries of the world began to grow again, their growth helped one another come out of the recession. The UK's economy is now fully recovered. Businesses are doing well, and more people have jobs. The UK's unemployment rate is currently very low at 4.3 percent (2017).

Recovery has been slow, but the United Kingdom has always been strong. Its economy has now gained back what it lost. More than anything else, its people are what make this nation able to overcome the challenges it faces.

EUROPEAN COUNTRIES TODAY: UNITED KINGDOM

ABOVE: *The pound sterling is the official currency of the United Kingdom. Along with the United States dollar, the euro, and the Japanese yen, sterling is one of the world's most important currencies traded on foreign exchange markets.*

Text-Dependent Questions

1. What did British people vote to do in a June 23, 2016, referendum?

2. Which political party did Tony Blair represent?

3. Why did the United Kingdom decide not to join the euro?

Research Project

Write a report on the reasons why the United Kingdom has a successful economy. Compare its economy with other European countries that are not as successful.

57

Words to Understand

Anglo-Saxon: A member of the German people who conquered England in the fifth century.

Multiculturalism: The preservation of different cultures or cultural identities within a country.

World Wide Web: A part of the Internet accessed and connected by hyperlinks.

BELOW: The Roman city of Bath is situated on the river Avon, in the west of England. It is considered to be one of the England's most beautiful cities.

Chapter Four
CITIZENS OF THE UNITED KINGDOM: PEOPLE, CUSTOMS & CULTURE

The people of the United Kingdom are known for their creativity, talent, and industriousness. After all, the British Isles were the birthplace of Newton, Darwin, Shakespeare, the Beatles, Eric Clapton, and the inventors of the hovercraft and the World Wide Web—not to mention J. K. Rowling, the author of the *Harry Potter* series.

Population Facts

In 2017, the United Kingdom's population was estimated at more than 64.7 million, making it the second largest in the EU and the twenty-first largest in the world. Its overall population density is one of the highest in the world. Almost one-third of the population lives in England's prosperous southeast, with about 8.63 million people in the capital city of London. The British are famous for being reserved in manners, dress, and speech. They are known around the world for their politeness, self-discipline, and their dry sense of humor.

Many of the people of the United Kingdom are descended mainly from the varied ethnic stocks that settled there before the eleventh century. After the Norman invasion, the pre-Celtic, Celtic, Roman, Anglo-Saxon, and Norse influences were blended with the culture of the Scandinavian Vikings who had lived in Northern France. Today, Celtic languages persist in Wales, Scotland, and Northern Ireland, but the predominant language is English, which is a blend of Anglo-Saxon and Norman French.

Modern Britain, however, has attracted immigrants from all over the world, and today it is a country of mixed cultures. London has the largest nonwhite population of any European city, with over 250 languages spoken there. Multiculturalism and a changing economy have gradually worn away the British class system, but features of the system remain.

CITIZENS OF THE UNITED KINGDOM: PEOPLE, CUSTOMS & CULTURE

What Is Social Class?

Sociologists define social class as the grouping of people in terms of wealth or status. In earlier centuries, Great Britain had sharply divided upper and lower classes; the upper class was the nobility, while members of the lower class were referred to as commoners.

In the twentieth century, British society was divided into three main groups: the upper class, the middle class, and the lower or working class. The upper classes tended to consist of people with inherited wealth, and included some of the oldest families, many of whom were aristocrats with titles (such as Sir or Lady). The upper classes were defined by their titles, but also by their education and their pastimes, which included the traditional sports of hunting, shooting, fishing, and horseback riding. The middle classes made up the majority of the population of Britain and included industrialists, professionals, businesspeople, and shop owners. Meanwhile, working-class people were mostly farmworkers, miners, or factory workers. The British could tell which class people belonged to by their accent, by their clothes, by the way that they educated their children, and even by their interests and the types of food they ate.

In today's United Kingdom, however, class is more apt to be based on occupation. From this perspective, doctors, lawyers, and university teachers are given higher status than unskilled laborers. The different positions represent different levels of power, influence, and money.

EUROPEAN COUNTRIES TODAY: UNITED KINGDOM

Religion

The Church of England and the Church of Scotland are the official churches in their respective parts of the country, but because the United Kingdom has such a large immigrant population, most religions found in the world are also represented in the United Kingdom.

Education

The United Kingdom is a nation steeped in tradition—but it is also very much part of the twenty-first century, thanks in large part to the excellence of its educational system. The nation's high literacy rate can be credited to the universal public education introduced for the primary level in 1870 and the secondary level in 1900. Today, education is mandatory from ages five through sixteen, and nearly half of British students go on to postsecondary education.

ABOVE: *The Shri Swaminarayan Mandir is a Hindu temple in Neasden, London. It was built using traditional methods and materials, and was completed in 1995.*

CITIZENS OF THE UNITED KINGDOM: PEOPLE, CUSTOMS & CULTURE

ABOVE: Clare and King's are colleges at Cambridge University, Cambridge, England. The University was founded in 1209 and is now rated one of the best universities in the world.

Food & Drink

Traditionally, the United Kingdom has not been famous for its fine cooking but for its plain, yet hearty, basic recipes, that generally consist of meat and root vegetables, with a heavy reliance on foods available from one season to another. Fish and chips has been a firm favorite using the accessible ingredients of fish and potatoes. Each country in the United Kingdom has variations on the main traditions. In Scotland, the cooking reflects local produce, relying on wild game, dairy, cereals, and fruit. Historically, the Welsh have been meat-lovers, with a strong tradition of raising animals. Northern Ireland is known or its love of fried food, soda breads, and potato recipes. Nowadays, however, chefs are making a feature of the United Kingdom's fresh and quality ingredients. High-end restaurants are springing up all over the country promoting British food.

EUROPEAN COUNTRIES TODAY: UNITED KINGDOM 🇬🇧

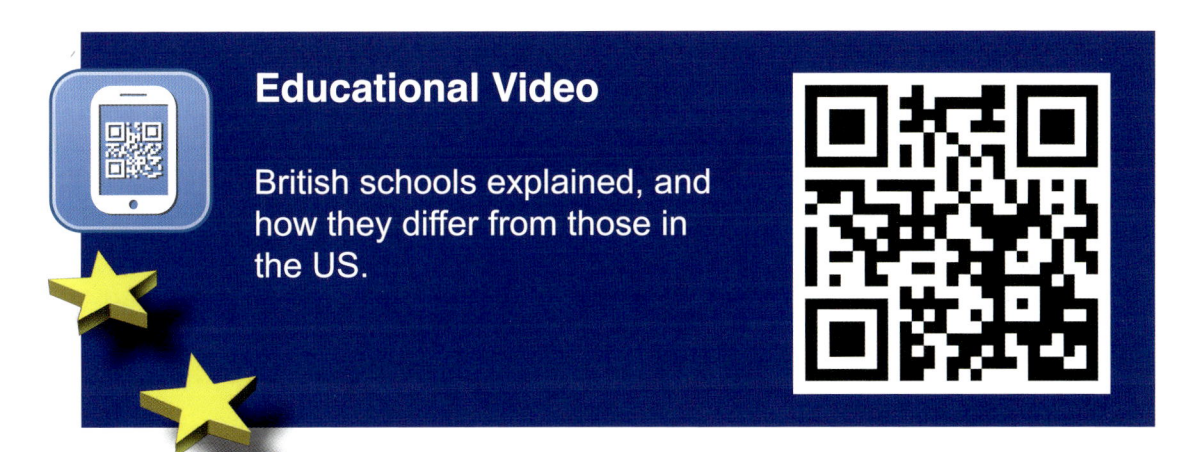

Educational Video

British schools explained, and how they differ from those in the US.

ABOVE: *A teacher with a class of primary school children. The children are educated at this level between the ages of five and twelve. A primary school is the British equivalent of an elementary school in the United States.*

🇬🇧 CITIZENS OF THE UNITED KINGDOM: PEOPLE, CUSTOMS & CULTURE

Britain, with its long history of immigration, is now home to cuisines from all over the world, and is a place where one can experience foods such as Chinese, Indian, Greek, Thai, and Middle Eastern cooking. These are available in most towns and cities across the country.

Britain has long had a tradition of brewing beer and has many famous breweries producing a whole range of products. Cider is produced in the west of England, whiskey in Scotland and Northern Ireland, and gin is made in many locations, but particularly in London. Britain also has a fledgling wine industry. Most vineyards are located in southern Britain where the weather is fine. The wines produced are of high quality and highly sought-after.

ABOVE: *Fish and chips is a traditional meal served all over the UK. Traditionally, it is eaten out of newspaper and in some regions, served with mushy peas.*

EUROPEAN COUNTRIES TODAY: UNITED KINGDOM

Yorkshire Pudding Popovers
(Traditionally made to accompany roast beef)

Makes 12

Ingredients
1 ¼ cups flour
½ teaspoon of salt
1 cup of milk
1 tablespoon melted butter
2 eggs
4 to 8 tablespoons of drippings from roasting pan

Directions
Whisk together the flour, salt, milk, butter, and eggs. Using a baster, drop a teaspoon or two of the drippings into each cup of a muffin tin. Put the muffin in a 450-degree oven. When the drippings are sizzling hot, remove the tin from the oven and fill each cup half or two-thirds full with the batter. Bake for 15 minutes, then reduce oven temperature to 350 degrees, and bake for 15 to 20 minutes longer, or until the popovers are puffed and brown.

Parkin
(Traditional cake from the north of England)

Ingredients
2 cups of flour
2 teaspoons of baking powder
2 teaspoons of ginger
½ cup sugar
1 cup of oats
1 cup of milk
⅓ cup of butter
1 cup of molasses and honey mixed

Directions
Preheat the oven to 325 degrees. Soak the oats in the milk for half an hour to soften. Melt the butter over a low heat and add the molasses and honey mixture. In a large bowl combine the flour, baking powder, ginger, and sugar. Combine molasses mixture and the oats (with any remaining milk) in another bowl, and add to the flour mixture. Pour into a 9- x 11-inch baking pan. Bake for 45 minutes or until the cake begins to come away from the sides of the pan.

🇬🇧 CITIZENS OF THE UNITED KINGDOM: PEOPLE, CUSTOMS & CULTURE

Literature

The United Kingdom has an important and rich cultural heritage. The English playwright and poet William Shakespeare is widely regarded as the greatest dramatist of all time.

In the nineteenth century, there followed fine writers including Jane Austen, the Brontë sisters, Charles Dickens, Thomas Hardy, the poet William Blake, and poet William Wordsworth. Twentieth century writers include H. G. Wells, D. H. Lawrence, Virginia Woolf, Evelyn Waugh, George Orwell, Graham Greene, J. R. R. Tolkien, and the poets John Betjeman and Ted Hughes. Scotland's contribution includes the writer Arthur Conan Doyle, Sir Walter Scott, and Robert Louis Stevenson. It has also produced the poet Robert Burns. More recently, Hugh

ABOVE: *William Shakespeare.*

ABOVE: *Jane Austen.*

ABOVE: *Sir Walter Scott.*

ABOVE: *J. K. (Joanna) Rowling.*

MacDiarmid and Neil M. Gunn contributed to what is known as the Scottish Renaissance in the first half of the twentieth century. Scotland's capital, Edinburgh, is UNESCO's first worldwide city of literature.

Welsh writers such as R. S. Thomas and Dylan Thomas have brought Welsh literature to an international audience.

Important writers and poets from Northern Ireland include Seamus Heaney, C. S. Lewis, Anna Burns, Brian Friel, John Hewitt, Louis MacNeice, and Gerard McKeown, to name but a few.

Art

The United Kingdom has produced many fine artists, a good example being the romantic landscape artist John Constable from Suffolk, who painted the *The Hay Wain*. Also from Suffolk was Thomas Gainsborough, who is famous for his society painting of the eighteenth century, as was Joshua Reynolds. Other celebrated painters from the United Kingdom are George Stubbs and Edwin Landseer, who painted animals with incredible detail and precision. Other greats include J .M. W. Turner, John Everett Millais, and William Holman Hunt of the Pre-Raphaelite movement and L. S. Lowery, famous for his stick people. The modern age has also produced some powerful artists, including Lucien Freud, Stanley Spencer, David Hockney, Damian Hurst, Tracey Emin and the mysterious Banksy.

Architecture

The United Kingdom has always been at the leading edge of architecture. From the earliest times, huge edifices have been constructed, such as Stonehenge during the Stone Age. In medieval times, masterpieces including St. Albans

ABOVE: Sir Christopher Wren.

CITIZENS OF THE UNITED KINGDOM: PEOPLE, CUSTOMS & CULTURE

Cathedral, with its Norman tower, and Westminster Abbey were built.

The Great Fire of London in 1666 gave rise to other prominent buildings, such as Christopher Wren's St. Paul's Cathedral. Other famous architectural works include the Circus in Bath, designed by John Wood the Elder, and Park Crescent in London, designed by John Nash.

Victorian Britain gave rise to great innovation and many important buildings such as the Royal Albert Hall, Manchester Town Hall, and Balmoral Castle.

One of Scotland's most famous architects is Charles Rennie Mackintosh whose most famous building is the Glasgow School of Art—which is currently undergoing restoration after a catastrophic fire in 2014.

ABOVE: The Circus in Bath, England, comprises three blocks of houses that form a circle. The houses were designed by John Wood the Elder. His son, John Wood the Younger, completed the work in 1768.

EUROPEAN COUNTRIES TODAY: UNITED KINGDOM

Into the modern era, the United Kingdom has produced some fine architects, such as Sir Norman Foster, who designed the Hong Kong and Shanghai Banking Corporation headquarters, the redesign and dome of the Reichstag in Berlin, and 30 St. Mary Axe (the Gherkin) in London. Another British great is Sir Richard Rogers, who designed the Millennium Dome and The Lloyd's Building in London, the European Court of Human Rights in Strasbourg, France, and Terminal 4 of Adolfo Suárez Madrid-Barajas Airport in Spain. Other notable architects include David Chipperfield, James Stirling, Tom Wright, and the late Zaha Hadid.

A Nation of Traditions

From Scotland to England, from Northern Ireland to the Channel Islands, the people of Great Britain love customs and traditions. Here are some of the strangest, oldest, and most interesting.

ABOVE: *The Gherkin is in the heart of the City of London's financial district. It was designed by Sir Norman Foster.*

Morris Dance Dating from fifteenth century, the Morris Dance is an ancient form of English folk dance accompanied by music. It is performed by a group of men who dance with rhythmical steps. They usually wearing bell pads on their shins. Implements such as sticks, swords, and handkerchiefs are wielded by the dancers. Traditionally, it is believed that the Morris Dance will bring good luck to the rural village where it is performed.

Up Helly Aa The Up Helly Aa Viking fire festival is held annually on the last Tuesday of January on the Shetland Islands in Scotland. Dating from the

CITIZENS OF THE UNITED KINGDOM: PEOPLE, CUSTOMS & CULTURE

ABOVE: *The Up Helly Aa festival is held every year in January at Lerwick on the island of Shetland.*

1880s, the festival is held to mark the end of the Yule season. The celebration begins as a procession of guizers (folk actors). In the larger towns, such as in Lerwick, the numbers taking part can be considerable. Smaller numbers march in the more rural areas. Marchers dress up in a variety of themed costumes, carry torches, and then set fire to a replica Viking ship.

Cheese Rolling Cheese Rolling is an annual event held on the Spring Bank Holiday at Cooper's Hill, near Gloucester in England. It is a tradition carried out by the people who live in the village of Brockworth. However, it has become so popular that it is now practiced by people all over the world. From the starting point at the top of the hill, a large round of Double Gloucester is sent hurtling down it. Then the competitors race down after it. It is spectacular to watch, but many competitors end up with broken arms and legs. The first person over the finish line at the bottom of the hill wins the cheese.

EUROPEAN COUNTRIES TODAY: UNITED KINGDOM

ABOVE: Revellers take part in the traditional cheese rolling races on Cooper's Hill, Brockworth, England. Thousands attend the event. It can be quite dangerous!

Text-Dependent Questions

1. How many languages are spoken in the United Kingdom?

2. Which architect designed]t. Paul's Cathedral in London?

3. When was the Great Fire of London?

Research Project

Write an essay on how the United Kingdom's culture has influenced the culture of North America.

Words to Understand

capital: A town or city that is the official seat of government in a country.

heritage: Something that has been handed down from the past.

metropolis: A very large, busy city.

BELOW: London is constantly changing as more cutting-edge architecture is commissioned. Blending in the old with the new, London's skyline is now quite spectacular.

Chapter Five
THE FAMOUS CITIES OF THE UNITED KINGDOM

The United Kingdom has only a few urban areas. With a population of nearly nine million people, London, the **capital** of the United Kingdom, is far larger than any other British city. Britain's only other city with a population of more than one million is the West Midlands community of Birmingham. Leeds, Manchester, Glasgow, Bradford, and Sheffield are smaller British cities, the only five with a population of more than 500,000 people.

London

People from many backgrounds flock to London looking for better jobs, a higher standard of living, and cultural opportunities. Not only citizens of the United Kingdom move to live here; the city also attracts immigrants from around the world. What's more, tourists are drawn to London's busy shops, its cultural riches, and its ancient historical **heritage**. Every year, more than 120 million people arrive or depart from one of London's airports. Heathrow, London's main airport, handles around 76 million passengers a year, making it one of the busiest and most connected airports in the world.

ABOVE: St. Paul's Cathedral, a masterpiece designed by Sir Christopher Wren.

73

THE FAMOUS CITIES OF THE UNITED KINGDOM

Residents of London frequently feel it is like an enormous collection of villages: although it is a bustling modern **metropolis**, clusters of local shops, markets, and parks and other leisure centers give it a strong feeling of local community. Some areas of the city have particularly strong ethnic identities.

Greater London covers an area of 612 square miles (1,584 sq. km), 1.2 percent of England's total land area. It has seventeen national museums and four World Heritage sites: the Palace of Westminster, the Tower of London, Maritime Greenwich, and Kew Gardens. London is also a very green city, with 147 registered parks and gardens, and eight royal parks. In fact, 30 percent of London's entire area is open space, which helps make it an inviting and beautiful city.

Birmingham

Birmingham may not be as beautiful as parts of London, but England's second-largest city has an important industrial legacy. World War II bombs left behind a grim atmosphere—but modern Birmingham has undergone a face-lift. The city's many canals offer developers sites

RIGHT: *The Changing of the Guard ceremony at Buckingham Palace, London. A "must-see" on a trip to London.*

74

EUROPEAN COUNTRIES TODAY: UNITED KINGDOM

THE FAMOUS CITIES OF THE UNITED KINGDOM

Educational Video

London Vacation Travel Guide. Visit the most famous sights of this great city.

ABOVE: *The Bullring shopping center is located in the commercial center of Birmingham. The Selfridges & Co. building's futuristic design is in stark contrast to many of the other buildings in the area.*

EUROPEAN COUNTRIES TODAY: UNITED KINGDOM

ABOVE: Old warehouses along the river Aire are a testament to Leeds's industrial past. Today, the buildings have been converted into luxury apartments, shops, and offices.

for trendy cafés. Birmingham is well-known for its large and lucrative shopping center, the Bullring. Today, Birmingham's economy is dominated by the service sector. Birmingham is also a major international commercial center. It is home to six universities and important cultural institutions, including the City of Birmingham Symphony Orchestra, the Birmingham Royal Ballet, the Library of Birmingham, and the Barber Institute of Fine Arts. Literary figures associated with the Birmingham area include Samuel Johnson, Arthur Conan Doyle, W. H. Auden, and J. R. R. Tolkien. It is the fourth most visited city in the UK by overseas visitors. The people of Birmingham are nicknamed "Brummies." There is a distinctive Brummie accent and dialect.

Leeds

The city of Leeds is located in West Yorkshire, England. Leeds has an ancient history dating back to the fifth century. It was also once a child of the textile industry. The industrial revolution increased its population nearly tenfold. Today, cloth production is nonexistent, and Leeds is no longer the industrial center it once was. However, the city is thriving and is now the second-largest

THE FAMOUS CITIES OF THE UNITED KINGDOM

information technology center in England. This vibrant urban community has undergone a successful transformation form a smoky factory town to a modern city packed with services, especially of the educational kind. The extensive retail area of Leeds is a regional shopping center for the whole of the Yorkshire and the Humber region. The large catchment area has given rise to hundreds of shops for visitors to choose from. Leeds is also the location of key government offices, such as the Department for Work and Pensions, the Department of Health, and Her Majesty's Revenue and Customs.

Sheffield

Sheffield, located in the county of South Yorkshire in the North of England, was first established as an Anglo-Saxon village. What was once a small clearing in the forest has since expanded to become a major city in England.

During the nineteenth century, Sheffield became one of Britain's leading industrial cities; today, it is still recognized for its important contributions to the United Kingdom's successful steel industry. Despite many of the steel firms being shut down after World War II, Sheffield produces more steel than ever

ABOVE: *Sheffield's historic center. The historic townhall is on the right.*

EUROPEAN COUNTRIES TODAY: UNITED KINGDOM

ABOVE: *The Winter Garden, Sheffield, is one of the largest temperate glasshouses to be built in the UK during the last hundred years, and the largest urban glasshouse anywhere in Europe.*

now. Inventions of new technologies and changes in market demands have kept the industry alive and well.

Sheffield has its five rivers to thank for much of its success, since these waterways have provided transportation to the city's industries. The city has also developed its tram service, with the most recent advancement being the introduction of the Supertrams in 1994, making Sheffield the proud owner of the nation's most advanced urban tram system. Today, Sheffield is a major industrial, cosmopolitan, and cultural center, renowned for its green open spaces, creative talents, galleries, sport facilities, and high-quality steel products. Sheffield is home to two universities (the University of Sheffield and Sheffield Hallam University). Both have excellent ratings in teaching and research and after students graduate, the town is an attractive place for them to settle in.

THE FAMOUS CITIES OF THE UNITED KINGDOM

Belfast

Belfast is the capital city of Northern Ireland. It is the second-largest city on the island of Ireland (Dublin in the Republic of Ireland is the largest). Belfast is situated at the mouth of the river Lagan on Belfast Lough. It is often associated with the Troubles that occurred from 1960 to 1977, when sectarian violence made certain parts of the city no-go areas. Following the signing of the Good Friday Agreement in 1998, the violence has stopped and now Belfast has become one of the safest cities in the UK. Today, Belfast is a wonderful city to visit and explore. It has changed dramatically over the last twenty years and is now prosperous and thriving. Belfast is famous for its cultural scene, with international artists and bands performing at venues like the Belfast Waterfront

ABOVE: *Belfast Castle is a tourist attraction on the slopes of Cavehill Country Park, Belfast.*

EUROPEAN COUNTRIES TODAY: UNITED KINGDOM

Titanic Belfast

Titanic Belfast is an important visitor attraction and experience that explores the Titanic story. It is also a monument to Belfast's maritime past. Titanic Belfast is located on the site of the former Harland & Wolff shipyard in the city's Titanic Quarter, where the famous RMS Titanic was built. The exhibition tells the story of the ill-fated Titanic, which hit an iceberg and sank during her maiden voyage in 1912. The building houses a series of galleries, private function rooms, and community facilities. Visitors can explore the very spot where the Titanic was launched.

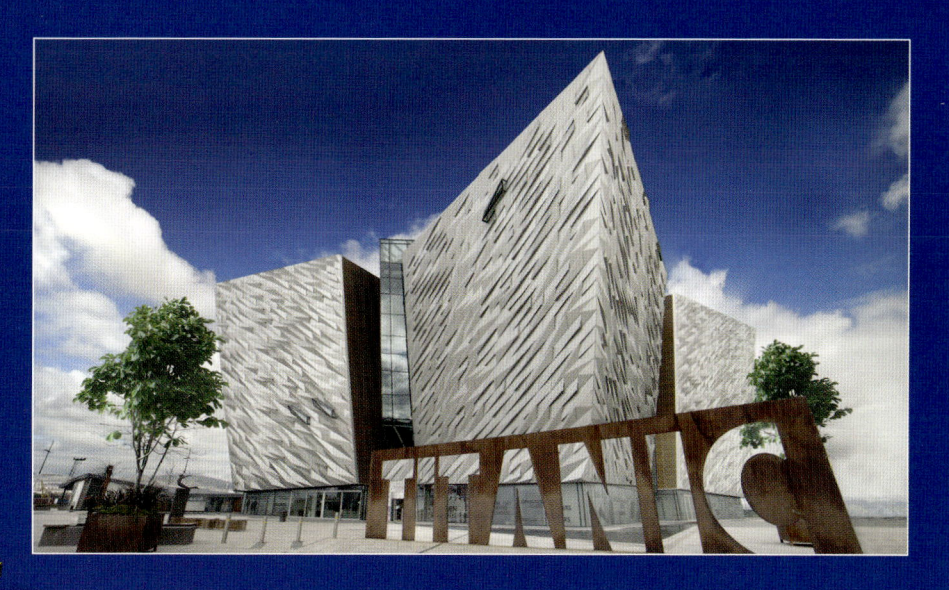

and the world-class Odyssey Arena. Visitors can also visit other cultural centers, scientific exhibitions, or explore Belfast's literary past. Some additional important destinations to visit are Titanic Belfast, the Giant's Causeway, Hillsborough Castle and Gardens, and Crumlin Road Gaol.

THE FAMOUS CITIES OF THE UNITED KINGDOM

Cardiff

Cardiff is the capital and the largest city in Wales. It is the commercial and cultural center of Wales and is also the base for the Welsh media and sporting institutions. It is also the seat of the Welsh National Assembly. Cardiff's rich culture has a diverse range of influences, from the Romans and Normans of antiquity to the industrial revolution and the coal industry—which transformed Cardiff from a small town into a thriving, international city. Today, Cardiff is a city

ABOVE: *The copper-roofed Millennium Centre in Cardiff, Wales.*

EUROPEAN COUNTRIES TODAY: UNITED KINGDOM

of many attractions. Choose from its historic houses and castles, or experience its surrounding countryside and wildlife. The city has a lively entertainment scene, where visitors can experience a range of arts, including opera, ballet, musicals, and live music venues. In addition, Cardiff has a range of galleries and museums to choose from. For those interested in the city itself, visitors can find out about Cardiff's local history at the Cardiff Story Museum.

🇬🇧 THE FAMOUS CITIES OF THE UNITED KINGDOM

Glasgow

The Scottish city of Glasgow is one of Britain's largest, liveliest, and most interesting cities, with appealing Victorian architecture, several museums, and a sense of history that carries visitors back into medieval times. The city grew from a small rural settlement on the river Clyde to become one of the most influential seaports in Britain. From the eighteenth century onwards, the city became the main transatlantic hub for trade with the West Indies and North America.

   In 1999, Glasgow followed up the European City of Culture award it had won almost a decade previously by serving as the United Kingdom's City of Architecture and Design. It offers important cultural attractions, including the Scottish Opera, the Scottish Ballet, the National Theatre of Scotland, the Royal

ABOVE: *Buchanan Street is a pedestrianized shopping area in Glasgow.*

EUROPEAN COUNTRIES TODAY: UNITED KINGDOM

Scottish National Orchestra, and the BBC Scottish Symphony Orchestra. The city is also home to many live music venues, pubs, and clubs.

Glasgow's economy is very important to Scotland. While manufacturing has declined, its economy has seen good growth in the tertiary sector: financial services, the creative industries, health care, higher education, and tourism are thriving. However, despite successes, the city must cope with a relatively low standard of living, housing problems for its inhabitants, and relatively high unemployment rates.

Text-Dependent Questions

1. How many of the United Kingdom's cities have populations of more than 500,000?

2. What county is Sheffield located in?

3. What is the name of the river that runs through Glasgow?

Research Project

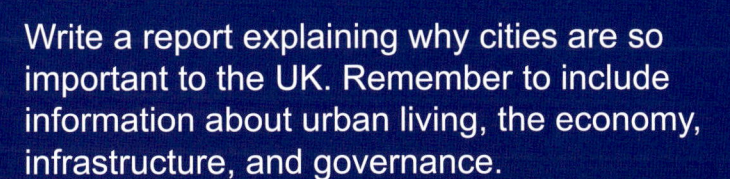

Write a report explaining why cities are so important to the UK. Remember to include information about urban living, the economy, infrastructure, and governance.

Words to Understand

economy: The process or system by which goods and services are produced, sold, and bought in a country.

natural gas: A flammable gas mixture from below the earth's surface that is used for fuel.

pharmaceuticals: Drugs or medicines.

BELOW: For such a small country, the United Kingdom is diverse and beautiful. Tourism is very important to its economy, bringing in billions of pounds every year.

Chapter Six
A BRIGHT FUTURE FOR THE UNITED KINGDOM

The United Kingdom is a leading trading power and is one of the most important financial centers in the world. It has the fifth-largest **economy** in the world. Following World War II, the UK invested heavily in agriculture, and therefore has one of the most efficient farming systems in Europe, producing about 50 percent of food needs with less than 2 percent of the labor force. The UK has abundant natural resources, including large coal, **natural gas**, and oil reserves. However, due to its oil and natural gas reserves declining, the UK is now a net importer of energy. Financial services, particularly banking and insurance, are key to the UK's economy. As in many advanced nations, manufacturing in the UK has declined, but it is still very important to the UK's GDP. Manufactured products include: mineral fuels and oil, nuclear reactors and parts, **pharmaceuticals**, electrical appliances, precious metals, aircraft, plastics, iron and steel, beverages, chemical products, published materials, and clothing, to name but a few.

ABOVE: *United Kingdom and EU flags.*

🇬🇧 A BRIGHT FUTURE FOR THE UNITED KINGDOM

Today, the UK is one of the fastest growing economies in the G7. However, economists and politicians are concerned about the negative effect of the UK's vote to leave the EU (Brexit). The UK has an important trade relationship with other EU members through its single market membership, and it is possible that Britain's potential exit from the EU will jeopardize its position as an important location for European and worldwide financial services.

ABOVE: *The United Kingdom is a world leader in science-based technology. Robotic engineering is one area where British design is cutting edge.*

EUROPEAN COUNTRIES TODAY: UNITED KINGDOM

Despite the uncertainty caused by the Brexit vote, the UK's economy is holding up, particularly as regards to consumer spending. However, it has been predicted that the economy will slow down from 1.8 percent in 2016 to 1.4 percent in 2018.

The housing market in the UK is likely to remain subdued in the next couple of years and interest rates will remain low.

The UK has always been a resourceful and adaptable nation and has accepted new challenges as they have arisen. Innovation, research and development, and education have helped drive the UK's economy. Even though it has its problems, the UK is on course for a successful future.

Text-Dependent Questions

1. What are natural resources?

2. What is the state of the United Kingdom's economy today?

3. Why is the UK's trading relationship with other EU countries currently in jeopardy?

Research Project

Write a report on the kinds of economic problems that advanced countries like the United Kingdom face in the future.

CHRONOLOGY

55 BCE Julius Caesar invades the British Isles.
43 CE Romans bring the British Isles into the Roman Empire.
330 Pytheas becomes the first person who can read and write to visit the British Isles.
410 Roman Empire withdraws from Britain.
597 St. Augustine comes to Britain as a missionary from Rome.
1066 William, Duke of Normandy, sails across the English Channel and conquers the Anglo-Saxons.
1215 King John is forced to sign the Magna Carta.
1485 The Wars of the Roses end.
1620 Pilgrims set out for the "New World."
1765 United Kingdom buys the Isle of Man.
1837 Queen Victoria assumes the throne.
1870 Universal public education is introduced for the primary level; it is extended to secondary level in 1900.
1914 Outbreak of World War I.
1921 Northern Ireland is allowed to have its own parliament; Southern Ireland breaks from the United Kingdom and becomes the Republic of Ireland.
1939 Outbreak of World War II.
1945 The UK becomes a permanent member of the UN Security Council.
1959 Britain joins in the creation of the European Free Trade Association.
1973 Britain joins the European Community.
1979 Margaret Thatcher becomes the first woman prime minister of Britain.
1999 The Good Friday Agreement brings an official end to the conflict in Northern Ireland.
2004 The EU expands to include Eastern European nations.
2008 Recession hits the entire world.
2014 Voters in a referendum in Scotland reject independence.
2016 Political crisis after voters in a referendum opt to quit the European Union. David Cameron resigns, succeeded by Theresa May.
2017 Formal negotiations begin to end Britain's membership of the European Union.

Further Reading

Leapman, Michael. *DK Eyewitness Travel Guide: Great Britain*. London: DK, 2016.

McCormick, John. *Understanding the European Union: A Concise Introduction*. London: Palgrave Macmillan, 2017.

Mason, David S. *A Concise History of Modern Europe: Liberty, Equality, Solidarity*. London: Rowman & Littlefield, 2015.

Steves, Rick. *Rick Steves Great Britain*. Edmonds: Rick Steves' Europe, Inc., 2016.

Internet Resources

Lonely Planet Great Britain

https://www.lonelyplanet.com/great-britain

Visit Britain

https://www.visitbritain.com

United Kingdom: Country Profile

http://www.bbc.co.uk/news/world-europe-18023389

United Kingdom: CIA World Factbook

https://www.cia.gov/library/publications/resources/the-world-factbook/geos/uk.html

The Official Website of the European Union

europa.eu/index_en.htm

Publisher's note:
The websites listed on this page were active at the time of publication. The publisher is not responsible for websites that have changed their addresses or discontinued operation since the date of publication. The publisher will review and update the website list upon each reprint.

INDEX

A
Aberdeenshire, 38
Act of Settlement, 36
AD (Anno Domini), 28
Adolfo Suárez Madrid-Barajas
 Airport, 69
Agriculture, 53–54, 55, 87
Aire river, 77
Alfred the Great, 30
Angles, 30
Anglican Church, 9, 33, 34
Anglo-Saxon
 language, 31, 59
 people, 30, 31, 59
Animals, 21, 22, 23, 24–25
Anne, Queen, 36
Archaeologist, 27
Architecture, 67–69
Art, 67
Auden, W. H., 77
Austen, Jane, 66
Austerity, 50
Australia, 36
 autonomy, 40
Avon river, 58
Axis forces, 41

B
Balmoral Castle, 37, 38, 68
Bamford Edge, 20
Bank of England, 48
Banksy, 67
Barber Institute of Fine Arts, 77
Bath, 58, 68
Battle of Hastings, 31
Bayeux Tapestry, 31
BC (Before Christ), 28
BCE (Before the Common Era), 28
Beaches, 19
Beatles, The, 59
Beer, 64
Belfast, 80–81
 Castle, 80
 Lough, 80
 Waterfront, 80
Belgium, 47, 55
Ben Nevis, 7, 17
Berlin, 69
Bermuda, 40
Betjeman, John, 66
Bevan, Aneurin, 41

Birds, 24
Birmingham, 74, 76, 77
 Royal Ballet, 77
Birth rate, 9
Blair, Tony, 41, 50
Blake, William, 66
Borderlands, 14
Borders, 7
Brexit, 56, 88, 89
British
 Commonwealth of Nations, 40
 Empire, 36, 39, 40
Brittany, 35
Brontë sisters, 66
Brown
 Gordon, 41
 John, 37
Brussels, 46
Buchanan Street, 84
Buckingham Palace, 38, 45, 74–75
Bullring shopping center, 76, 77
Burns
 Anna, 67
 Robert, 66

C
Caesar, Julius, 28
Cambridge, 62
 University, 62
Cameron, David, 41
Canada, 12, 36
 autonomy, 40
Capital, 49, 50, 73
Cardiff, 82–83
 Story Museum, 83
Cavehill Country Park, 80
CE (Common Era), 28
Celtic languages, 59
Celts, 27, 59
Changing of the Guard ceremony, 74–75
Charles
 II, 34
Cheese Rolling, 70, 71
China, 55
Chipperfield, David, 69
Christianity, 9, 30, 31
Churchill, Winston, 40
Church of
 England, 61
 Scotland, 61

Cider, 64
Cities, 73–85
Clapton, Eric, 59
Clare and King's colleges, 62
Class system, 59, 60
Climate, 7, 8, 18–20, 27
Clyde river, 84
Coal, 52, 87
Coastline, 12
Colonies, 36, 40
Common law, 41
Commonwealth, 40
Conservative parties, 41
Constable, John, 67
Constitution, 41
Cooper's Hill, 70, 71
Cornish language, 9
Cornwall, 11, 30
County
 Antrim, 17
 Down, 18
Covent Garden, 8
Cromer, 19
Crumlin Road Gaol, 81
Currency, 47, 54, 55, 57

D
Dance, 69
Darwin, 59
Dating systems, 28
Deficit, 51
Democracy, 36
Denmark, 30
Dickens, Charles, 66
Downing Street, 44
Doyle, Arthur Conan, 66, 77

E
Economy, 49–57, 59, 88
 recession, 56
Edinburgh, 67
 Castle, 15
Education, 36, 61, 63
 postsecondary, 61
 primary school, 61, 63
Edward
 I (Edward Longshanks), 32
 VII, 36
Egypt, 39
Elections, 43
Elevation, 7

92

INDEX

Elizabeth
    II, 38, 45
    I (Virgin Queen), 33, 35
Emin, Tracey, 67
Empire, 36
Energy, 52
England, 8, 12–14, 19, 22, 26, 30, 35, 53, 58, 62, 64, 70, 71, 77, 78
English
    Channel, 27, 30–31
    language, 59
Ethnic groups, 9
Eurasian red squirrel, 21
Euro, 47, 54, 55
European
    Central Bank, 51
    City of Culture, 84
    Coal and Steel Community, 47
    Community, 47
    Court of Human Rights, 69
    Economic and Monetary Union (EMU), 54–55
    Economic Community, 47
European Union (EU), 18
    autonomy, 46, 47
    Brexit, 51, 56, 88, 89
    flag, 87
    formation, 46–47
    members, 46, 47
    Parliament Building, 46
    single market, 47
Exports, 55

F
Falkland Islands, 40
Far East, 36
Farming, 53
Farne Islands, 24
Fens, the, 7, 23
Fertility rate, 9
Financial services, 87
Firth of Forth, 49
Fish and chips, 62, 64
Flag, 8, 87
Flora and fauna, 21–25
Folklore, 11
Food and drink, 62, 64–65
Forests, 21–23
Fort William, 17
Foster, Sir Norman, 68
France, 7, 27, 30–31, 35, 46, 47, 55, 59, 69
French language, 31
Freud, Lucien, 67
Friel, Brian, 67

G
Gainsborough, Thomas, 67
Gas, 52, 87
Geography, 7
    and landscape, 11–26
Germany, 30, 51, 55
Gherkin (30 St. Mary Axe), 69
Giant's Causeway, 17, 81
Gibraltar, 40
Gin, 64
Glaciers, 27
Glasgow, 84–85
    School of Art, 68
Glasshouse, 79
Glenfinnan Viaduct, 16
Glen More (the Great Glen), 17
Good Friday Agreement, 80
Government, 27–48
Grangemouth Refinery, 49
Great
    Britain, 35
    Fire of London, 68
Greene, Graham, 66
Gross domestic product (GDP), 51, 52, 53, 55
    per capita, 55
Guizers, 69–70
Gunn, Neil M., 67

H
Hadid, Zaha, 69
Hadrian's Wall, 29
Hampshire, 22
Hanover, House of, 36
Hardy, Thomas, 66
Harry Potter, 59
    movies, 16
Hawes, 13
Hay Wain, The (Constable), 67
Hazards, 7
Heaney, Seamus, 67
Heathrow, 73–74
Hedgehogs, 25
Henry
    I, 32
    II, 32
    VII, 33
    VIII, 33
Hewitt, John, 67
Highlands, 16, 17
Hinduism, 9, 61
History, 27–48
Hockney, David, 67
Hong Kong and Shanghai Banking Corporation headquarters, 68
House of
    Commons, 42, 43
    Lords, 42, 43–44
Hovercraft, 59
Hughes, Ted, 66
Hunt, William Holman, 67
Hurst, Damian, 67
Hussein, Saddam, 41

I
Immigrants, 11, 27, 59, 61, 64, 73–74
Imports, 55
India, 36, 39
    independence, 40
Industrial revolution, 36, 77
Industry, 53, 55
Infant mortality rate, 9
Information technology, 78
Inverness, 17
Ireland, 7, 55
Ireland (Republic of Ireland), 7, 18, 34
    independence, 39
Irish
    language, 9
    Sea, 20
Islam, 9
Islands, 8, 12, 20, 24
Isle of Wight, 20
Italy, 47

J
Jacobite Steam Train, 16
James
    I, 33, 35
    IV, 35
    VI, 35
Johnson, Samuel, 77
Judiciary, 41, 44
Jutes, 30

93

INDEX

K
Kew Gardens, 74
King Arthur, 11
King John, 31

L
Labour party, 41, 50
Lackland, John, 32
Lagan river, 80
Lake District, 10, 14
    National Park, 10
Lakes, 10, 17, 18
Landseer, Edwin, 67
Language, 9, 59
Lawrence, D. H., 66
Leeds, 77–78
Lerwick, 69–70
Lewis, C. S., 67
Library of Birmingham, 77
Life expectancy, 9
Literacy rate, 61
Literature, 66–67
Loch Ness Monster, 11
Lochs, 17
London, 8, 36, 43, 44, 48, 49, 50, 61, 64, 68, 69, 73–74
    population, 59
    skyline, 72
    Stock Exchange, 48
Lough Neagh, 18
Lowery, L. S., 67
Lowlands, 14
Luxembourg, 47

M
Maastricht Treaty, 47
MacDiarmid, Hugh, 66–67
Mackintosh, Charles Rennie, 68
MacNeice, Louis, 67
Magna Carta, 31
Major, John, 41
Manchester Town Hall, 68
Manufacturing, 39, 87
Map, 6
Maritime Greenwich, 74
Mary, Queen of Scots, 35
May, Theresa, 41, 44
Mayflower, 35
McKeown, Gerard, 67
Merger Treaty, 47
Middle
    Ages, 31–32
    East, 36
Millais, John Everett, 67
Millennium
    Centre, 82
    Dome, 69
Ministers, 42
Monarchy, 42
    role of, 42, 43
Morris Dance, 69
Mountains, 12, 14, 18
Mount Snowdon, 14
Mourne mountains, 18
Multiculturalism, 59
Mythology, 11

N
Nash, John, 68
National
    Health Service, 41
    Theatre of Scotland, 84
Nationalism, 39
Nations, 12
Netherlands, 47, 55
New
    Forest National Park, 22
    World, 35
Newton, Isaac, 59
New Zealand, 36
    autonomy, 40
Norfolk, 19
Normandy, 31
Norman French language, 59
Normans, 30–31, 59
Norse people, 59
North
    America, 11, 33
    Atlantic Current, 19
    Atlantic Drift, 8
    Atlantic Ocean, 7
    Channel, 17
    Sea, 7, 29, 30, 49
    Yorkshire, 13
Northern Ireland, 8, 12, 17–18, 59, 62, 64, 80
    writers, 67
Northumberland, 24

O
Odyssey Arena, 81
Oil, 49, 52, 87
Orwell, George, 66

P
Pakistan, independence, 40
Palace of Westminster, 74
Park Crescent, 68
Parkin, 65
Parks, 74
Parliament, 35, 38, 43
    Houses of, 43
    powers of, 41–42
    Scottish, 35
Peak District National Park, 20
Pennines mountains, 12, 14
Pennine Way, 13
People, 9, 59–71
    characteristics, 59
Pharmaceuticals, 87
Picts, 20
Pilgrims, 33, 34
Pixies, 11
Political parties, 41
Population, 9, 59
    age, 9
    growth rate, 9
Pound sterling, 55, 57
Pre-Raphaelite movement, 67
Presbyterian, 9
Prime minister, 41, 43, 44
Protestantism, 36
    and monarchy, 346
Puffins, 24
Pytheas, 27

R
Rainfall, 19
Recipes, 65
Records, written, 27
Religion, 9, 61
Reynolds, Joshua, 67
Richard the Lionheart, 32
RMS Titanic, 81
Robert the Bruce, 32
Robin Hood, 11
Rogers, Richard, 69
Roman
    Catholicism, 9, 34
    Empire, 28–30
Romans, 27, 59
    invasion, 28–30
Roosevelt, Franklin D., 40
Rowling, J. K., 59, 66
Royal Albert Hall, 68

INDEX

Royal Scottish National Orchestra, 84–85

S
Salisbury Plain, 26
Saxons, 30
Scafel Pike, 10
Scotland, 8, 12, 14–17, 30, 32–33, 35, 37, 38, 49, 59, 62, 64, 69–70, 84, 85
    writers, 66–67
Scots, 32
    language, 9
Scott, Sir Walter, 66
Scottish
    Gaelic, 9
    Opera, 84
    Renaissance, 67
Scrooge, Ebenezer, 11
Seasons, 19
Selfridges & Co., 76
Shakespeare, William, 11, 51, 59, 66
Sheffield, 78–79
    Hallam University, 79
Shetland Islands, 69–70
Shri Swaminarayan Mandir, 61
Slavery, 36
Snowdonia National Park, 14
Snowdon Mountain Railway, 14
Social class. *See* Class system
Socialism, 49
Solway Firth, 29
South
    Down, 18
    Wales, 52
    Yorkshire, 78
Spencer, Stanley, 67
Sperrins, 18
Sports, 36
St.
    Albans Cathedral, 67–68
    Augustine, 30
    George of England, 8
    Margaret's Church, 13
    Patrick of Ireland, 8
    Paul's Cathedral, 68, 73–74
Stalin, Joseph, 40
Stevenson, Robert Louis, 66
Stewart, 35
Stirling
    Castle, 32–33, 35
    James, 69
Stone Age, 27, 67
Stonehenge, 26, 27, 67
Strangford Lough, 18
Strasbourg, 69
Stratford-upon-Avon, 51
Stuart, Henry, 35
Stuarts, 35, 36
Stubbs, George, 67
Suffolk, 67
Supertrams, 79
Switzerland, 55

T
Tata Steel Plant, 52
Taxes, 49
Technology, 88
Thames river, 43
Thatcher, Margaret, 41, 42
Thomas
    Dylan, 67
    R. S., 67
Tintagel Castle, 11
Titanic Belfast, 81
Tolkien, J. R. R., 66, 77
Tourism, 16, 73–74, 86
Tower of London, 74
Traditions, 69–71
Treaties of Rome, 47
Treaty of Paris, 47
Troubles, 80
Tudors, 32–33, 35
Turner, J. M. W., 67
Tyne river, 29

U
Unemployment, 55, 56
UNESCO World Heritage list, 17, 67, 74
Unification of England and Scotland, 35
United
    Kingdom Overseas Territories, 41
    Kingdom's City of Architecture and Design, 84
    States, 12, 41, 55
University of Sheffield, 79
Up Helly Aa festival, 69–70

V
Victoria, Queen, 36–38
Victorian age, 36–38
Vikings, 30–31, 59
Virginia, 33

W
Wales, 8, 12, 14, 26, 30, 52, 53, 59, 62, 82
    writers, 67
Wallace, William, 32
War of the Roses, 32
Wastwater, 10
Waugh, Evelyn, 66
Wells, H. G., 66
Welsh
    language, 9
    National Assembly, 82
West
    Coast Railways, 16
    Germany, 46, 47
    Yorkshire, 77
Westminster, 35
    Abbey, 68
Whiskey, 64
William
    the Conqueror, 31
    Duke of Normandy, 31
    II, 31
Wiltshire, 26
Winchester, 30
Windsor Castle, 38
Wine, 64
Winter Garden, 79
Wood
    the Elder, John, 68
    the Younger, John, 68
Woolf, Virginia, 66
World War
    I, 39
    II, 41, 46, 74, 78, 87
World Wide Web, 59
Wren, Sir Christopher, 67, 68, 73–74
Wright, Tom, 69

Y
Yalta Conference, 40
Yorkists, 32
Yorkshire Pudding Popovers, 65

Picture Credits

All images in this book are in the public domain or have been supplied under license by © Shutterstock.com. The publisher credits the following images as follows:

Page 8: Pajor Pawel, page 17: S-F, page 19: Daniel Gale, page 44: Twocoms, page 45: Lorna Roberts, page 46: Roman Yanushevsky, page 50: Stephen Bures, page 51, 76: Claudio Divizia, page 52: Leighton Collins, page 54: Anna Levin, page 60: Mr Pics, page 61: Ron Ellis, page 66 below: JStone, page 69: Dan Breckwoldt, page 71: 1000 Words, page 75: Alex Segre, page 78: Lucian Milasan, page 79 Travellight, page 81 Atmosphere1, page 84: Cornfield.

Wikimedia Commons and the following:
page 42 above: OGL3, page 42 below: Chris Collins.

To the best knowledge of the publisher, all images not specifically credited are in the public domain. If any image has been inadvertently uncredited, please notify the publisher, so that credit can be given in future printings.

Video Credits

Page 12 CGP Grey: http://x-qr.net/1E8K
page 53 UK Trade & Investment (UKTI): http://x-qr.net/1D07
page 63 Anglophenia: http://x-qr.net/1FBM
page 76 Expedia: http://x-qr.net/1Ddu

Author

Dominic J. Ainsley is a freelance writer on history, geography, and the arts and the author of many books on travel. His passion for traveling dates from when he visited Europe at the age of ten of with his parents. Today, Dominic travels the world for work and pleasure, documenting his experiences and encounters as he goes. He lives in the south of England in the United Kingdom with his wife and two children.